DESSERTS WITH A DIFFERENCE

DESSERTS WITH

Carrot Cake, Fennel Tart, and

A DIFFERENCE

Other Surprising and Delicious Vegetable Desserts

SALLY AND MARTIN STONE

CLARKSON POTTER/PUBLISHERS
NEW YORK

ALSO BY SALLY AND MARTIN STONE

The Mustard Cookbook

Classic Mexican Cooking

The Brilliant Bean

The Essential Root Vegetable Cookbook

Published by Clarkson N. Potter, Inc., 201 East 50th Street, New York, New York 10022. Member of the Crown Publishing Group.
Random House, Inc. New York, Toronto, London, Sydney, Auckland

CLARKSON N. POTTER, POTTER, and colophon are trademarks of Clarkson N. Potter, Inc.

Manufactured in the United States of America
Design by Beth Tondreau Design

LIBRARY OF CONGRESS CATALOGING-IN-PUBLICATION DATA
Stone, Sally.
     Desserts with a difference : carrot cake, fennel tart, and other
surprising and delicious vegetable desserts / Sally and Martin
Stone.—1st ed.
     Includes index.
     1. Desserts.   2. Cake.   3. Cookery (Vegetables)   I. Stone,
Martin.   II. Title.
TX773.S873   1993
641.8′6—dc20   93–6566
                                                         CIP

ISBN 0-517-88072-5

10   9   8   7   6   5   4   3   2   1
FIRST EDITION

TO OUR BURGEONING FAMILY ON BOTH COASTS

CONTENTS

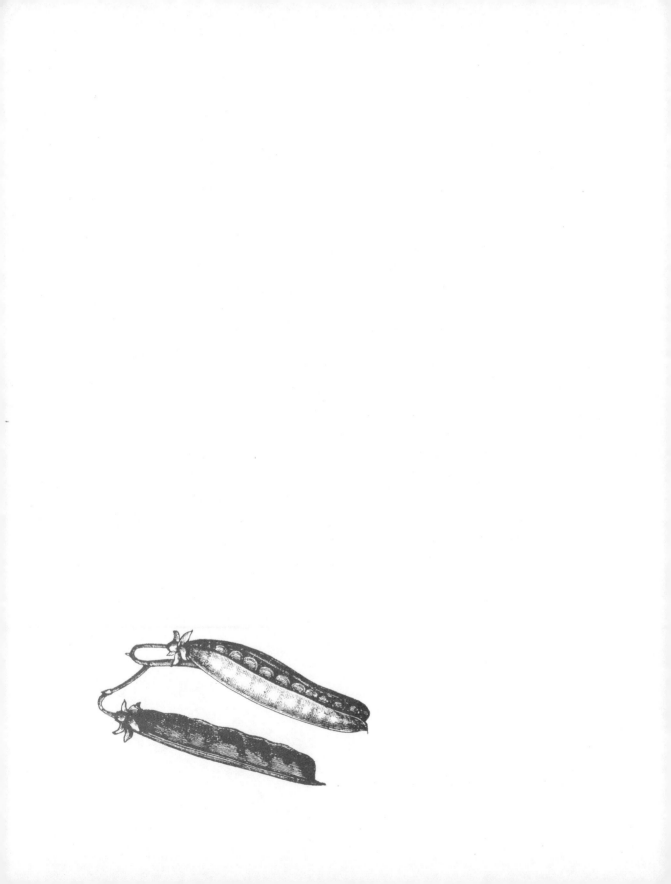

INTRODUCTION

We're out to change the way you think about the last—and what most people consider the best—course of a meal.

Parents used to say, "Eat your vegetables or you get no dessert!" Psychologically speaking, we now understand that this was the wrong tack; all that kids learn from this is that if it's good for them it can't taste good.

And of course nothing could be further from the truth. Fresh, in season, picked at the peak of ripeness, nothing could be more flavorful, more satisfyingly earthy, add more color, texture (not to mention nutrition) to a dish—even a dessert—than vegetables. The real problem is that most cooks don't know how to cook vegetables. Consequently, they often *don't* taste as good as they should.

As far as nutrition and healthful eating are concerned, we consider them absolutely essential parts of our daily lives—that's what inspired us to add vegetables to the dessert course of our meals in the first place. And just as good taste can cause one to make the wrong choices of what to eat, good taste can make one eat more of the things that are good for you. That's what this book is all about—making good things taste even better. No matter how good vegetables are for you, if they're not good tasting, what's the point? And when we put flavor first, nutrition—because of the vegetables in every recipe—becomes an unexpected and very welcome bonus.

Dessert, we feel, is an inalienable right. And vegetables just make it more right, a virtually justifiable obsession.

UNEXPECTED BUT NOT UNPRECEDENTED

When you first go through this book you might think it's just another case of creative cooks (the immodest way we think of ourselves) going off the deep end. But if people could set aside their preconceptions for a moment they would realize that vegetable desserts are not completely unheard of.

Besides the obvious examples of carrot cake and pumpkin pie, history does contain more than a few examples of how vegetables can work deliciously well in sweet preparations. In the Middle Ages, when sugar was expensive, scarce, and not in general use, parsnips were more often eaten as a sweet than as a vegetable. The American Indians introduced settlers to corn and the incomparable Indian pudding was born. Beets are not relished as a vegetable in Italy but the fresh greens find their way into a creamy, vanilla-scented cheesecake (the roots turn up in all their magenta glory, you will discover, in another cheesecake of our invention). Zucchini, perhaps out of a cook's desperate need to exhaust the overproduction of a home garden, was transformed ages ago into a delicious sweet tea bread. Almost any vegetable, we have found, can be converted into colorful desserts, moist baked goods, and other sweets that are both mouth-watering and more nourishing than their fruit and nut, flour, sugar, and egg forebears.

Because vegetables scarcely exist in the classic dessert repertoire, the vast majority of the recipes you'll discover in this book have no counterparts anywhere else. And as far as we know they have never been attempted before. They'll be completely new to you, just as they were to us.

Without question, our primary objective in creating these new recipes was that each and every dessert meet stringent flavor standards—ours. The next requirement, of almost equal importance, was that the recipes perform as conceived: in the oven, on the stove, on the plate or serving dish, on fork or spoon, even on the shelf, and, most important, on the tongue. When we tried them on family and friends, we were never satisfied with responses such as "good" or "okay" or even "interesting." The recipes couldn't be merely a rehash of some tried-and-true classic with a handful of grated carrots thrown in. They had to be *sensational*. Our aim was to create inventive, ingenious, original, and, as they say on Madison Avenue, lip-smacking good desserts. We wanted them to be in the best traditions of American and international cooking, yet trendsetting. We wanted them to be natural, not contrived, recognizable if not immediately identifiable. And, of course, delectable.

We found many of our best inspirations in classic vegetable side dish combinations. For example, Mexican jicama sticks spritzed with fresh lime juice and dusted with a little chile powder is a snack we loved in Mexico. We devised a jicama and lime cream pie that is true to the spirit of the original, even down to the addition of chile powder, that surprises, even shocks, yet pleases the tastebuds. The dessert never fails to bring back sweet memories of mariachi bands, colorful pottery, Mayan pyramids, and sumptuous seaside resorts.

When in Rome, you may have done as the Romans do, adding Sambuca to your after-dinner coffee. The licorice-flavored liqueur and coffee combo stimulated the creation of several desserts like our espresso cheesecake marbled with a flourish of sweetened fennel puree.

CHOOSING FROM THE GREENGROCER'S BINS

We have not used the full vegetable repertoire in this book. Nor is our list of vegetable desserts intended to be complete—there are hundreds more still to be invented, by us and others. Here we have adhered pretty much to those vegetables that are naturally sweet to begin with, such as carrots, parsnips, beets, Swiss chard; have a distinctive flavor, such as the licoricelike taste of fennel; or have special properties (the starchiness of beans, potatoes, Jerusalem artichokes) or textures.

We have taken liberties with the use of some ingredients like tomatoes, fresh and sun-dried. People have called tomatoes vegetables and used them as vegetables for so long that they have been treated as vegetables rather than the fruit they really are botanically. For the purposes of this book, we are considering them vegetables as well. Rice, too, is dealt with as a vegetable like potatoes, rather than a grain (which allowed us to invent dessert risottos made with fruit juices and fruit instead of broth and meats, fish, or poultry). Corn, another grain, is also served universally as a vegetable, so it turns up in this book in sweet concoctions, like a filling for chocolate crepes.

Take one of our inventions we like a lot: Acorn Squash Ginger Cream Log. This jellyroll–style dessert is made with a batter of pureed baked acorn squash, eggs, spices, and sugar baked as a sheet soufflé, spread with a filling of whipped cream blended with minced crystallized ginger, rolled, then dusted with a snowy drift of confectioners' sugar. A slice allows the mouth and tongue to experience the ecstasy of something melting, luscious, silken, and light all at once. We have also made this elegant finale with pureed pumpkin, zucchini, sweet potatoes, carrots, and parsnips (not all in the same recipe, but individually, at different times). In any of these incarnations we defy you—or your guests—to identify the main ingredient. That's not the point, of course. It's just that no one will *believe* the main ingredient is a vegetable and that such a rich, luxurious dessert could also be in any way nutritious.

This is not a gimmick cookbook, nor does it recklessly shoehorn its unusual (for this category) ingredients into a classification that does not fit. *Everything works*—to enhance either flavor or texture, to prolong shelf life, add moistness, and always to strengthen nutrition. *Everything works*—to produce a collection of desserts that are astonishingly delicious, much more healthful—and completely legitimate.

But don't expect fewer calories. These are desserts, after all. Rewards. Of course you can significantly whittle away the calorie and fat content of these recipes by making judicious substitutions for butter, cream, eggs, and sugar, but be aware that something will be lost in the translation. It's the price you must pay. You'll get all the vitamins, minerals, and fiber of the originals, all the good nutrition. But cutting down on fats and calories, more than likely, will cut down on flavor. We hate to say it, but it's true.

While we're on the subject of diets and health, let's talk for a moment about those fats. We use butter and cream in our recipes to make them sumptuous. But they are heavily weighted with a reputation, well deserved, for clogging some people's arteries.

One thing we wish you would remember: just because a cake might be made with 1 stick (¼ pound) of butter, a pair of eggs, and a cup of sugar doesn't mean that a serving will contain a huge quantity of fat, cholesterol, and calories. If you divide the offending fat, eggs, and sugar in a recipe by the number of portions we suggest it serves (and our portions are very generous), you often find that the fat, egg, and sugar content per portion is moderately low. If a cake made with a stick of butter serves 8, each suggested serving contains only 1 tablespoon of butter, or about 100 calories and 11 grams of fat. Do the same division with sugar and you discover that you are eating no more than a teaspoon or two at most. A couple of eggs means only a fraction of one egg per portion. Cut the slices thinner and you consume even less.

This is not discussed as a rationalization for gorging on desserts. Quite the contrary. If you, your family, or your guests have a problem with weight or cholesterol, make substitutions for the offending ingredients, of course, take only tiny portions, if you must—or just read this book and envy those who can eat from it worry-free. And don't forget, you can always save at least part of the ration of the eggs, sugar, and fat you *are* allowed (and most restricted diets allow some) for dessert, even if it just amounts to a forkful or spoonful once in a while. We are not advocates of complete deprivation. Deprivation can lead to secret cravings and subsequent closet fulfillment. We suggest moderation, restraint, and discretion.

Even though we invented them, we often found these new recipes to be a revelation, a surprise—startlingly *better* than we had ever anticipated. We never expected that employing vegetables for flavoring cakes, pies, and other sweets could produce desserts rivaling and even surpassing many standards. However, any reservations we had when testing—fears that a particular vegetable would not adapt perfectly to the dessert cart, would not offer the proper depth and subtlety—always seemed to vanish with the very first bite.

Even so, weaning our national sweet tooth away from traditional ideas of saving the best for last is no mean accomplishment—especially when the deviation from the norm involves a food most people, having begun the practice early in childhood, usually leave uneaten on their plates. But we think it's worth raising a few eyebrows and shaking up a few preconceived notions about what constitutes a dessert to get vegetables back in the mainstream of the American diet—right where they have always belonged.

In many ways this book was a natural outgrowth of a theme fundamental to all our cookbooks: *we are champions of the underutilized ingredient.* From mustard (our first cookbook elevated mustard from mere condiment to a versatile seasoning) to beans and root vegetables (neither thought of as chic, both dismissed as peasant foods), we have tried to find new uses for these underemployed (often *un*employed) ingredients in American kitchens. In our cookbooks these underdogs always seem to make it to the top. We hope we've done it again. We believe we have—so much so that now we wonder why no one ever thought of making desserts with vegetables before.

CAKES AND CHEESECAKES

These are not cakes your grandmother made. These are completely new—or such complete rethinkings of the tried-and-true that, to paraphrase that disclaimer at the end of every movie, "any resemblance to cakes you've ever eaten before is purely coincidental."

We offer for your approval twenty-nine recipes for layer cakes, pound cakes, loaf cakes, angel food cakes, strudels, and cake rolls all containing vegetables of one sort or another. Some are made with flour in the traditional way. Others substitute mashed potatoes, bean puree, beets, artichokes, Jerusalem artichokes, parsnips, or carrots for all or most of the flour found in conventional batters. They are all uncommon in two ways: uncommonly good and uncommonly novel.

The cheesecakes are so easy to make that we're always embarrassed when guests are overenthusiastic in their appreciation of what, to us, seems a minor effort. The only struggle we have is choosing what to flavor them with. Vegeta-

bles have been a boon to our growing list of fillings. Our hands-down favorite is ginger, but beet (actually our own beet jam) is running a close second. You'll also discover fennel and beet greens. Each lends its own distinctive flavor, texture, color (the deep purple / red color of beet jam marbled against snowy white is especially pleasing), and nourishment to this sophisticated and refreshing meal conclusion.

Cheesecakes freeze well so you can make them one or more weeks in advance. To freeze a cheesecake, remove it from its pan only after allowing it to cool for several hours, preferably overnight. Transfer it to a round of stiff cardboard covered with foil; wrap closely first in plastic wrap, then in freezer paper. Freeze for up to 6 weeks. Allow at least 2 hours to thaw and serve at room temperature or slightly chilled.

Incidentally, we defy any child ever again to refuse to eat his vegetables—in this form.

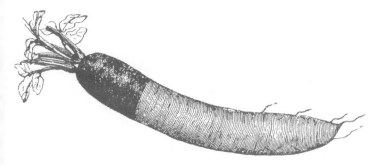

CAKES ■ *Classic Carrot Cake Updated* ■ *Heart of Artichoke Spice Cake* ■ *Pumpkin Pound Cake with Three Liqueurs* ■ *Aromatic Spiced Parsnip Bundt Cake* ■ *Sweet Potato and Walnut Coffee Cake* ■ *Spiced Zucchini Tea Loaves* ■ *Marbled Fennel Coffee Cake with Sambuca Espresso Glaze* ■ *Basic Chickpea Flourless Cake* ■ *Spicy Pinto Bean Fruit and Nut Cake* ■ *Orange Cream Garbanzo Bean Layer Cake* ■ *Red Bean Devil's Food Cake with Cocoa-Cream Icing* ■ *Fresh Tomato Date and Nut Spice Cake with Vanilla Cream Cheese Frosting* ■ *Cannellini Cloud Cake* ■ *Tomato Surprise Four-Layer Cake with Coconut Sour Cream Frosting* ■ *Gingery Fresh Gingerroot Gingerbread* ■ *Cream Cheese-Chickpea-Hazelnut Pound Cake* ■ *Double Demon Ginger Pound Cake* ■ *Carrot and Banana Coffee Cake* ■ *Fresh Ginger*

Angel Food Cake with Gingered Bittersweet Chocolate Frosting ■ *Beet-Apple-Ginger Upside-Down Cake* ■ *Carrot Cake Studded with Nuts and Apricots Cloaked in Orange Glaze* ■ *Gâteau Topinambour, or Jerusalem Artichoke Chocolate Cake* ■ *Brandied Chocolate Cake with Sun-Dried Tomatoes and Pecans* ■ *Sauerkraut Buttermilk Chocolate Layer Cake with White-on-White Icing* ■ *Moist Mashed Potato Chocolate Cake* ■ *Sweet and Flaky Swiss Chard Phyllo Roll with Raisins and Pine Nuts* ■ *Mexican Jalapeño Chocolate Cream Cake* ■ *Acorn Squash Ginger Cream Log* ■ *Delicately Spiced Zucchini Cream Roll*

CHEESECAKES ■ *1-2-3-4 Ginger Cheesecake* ■ *Espresso Fennel Cheesecake* ■ *Unbeetable Marbleized Orange Cheesecake* ■ *Italian Beet Green Cheesecake*

CLASSIC CARROT CAKE UPDATED

Serves 10 to 12

*t*his is our version of the classic carrot cake with cream cheese frosting. Most carrot cakes are so predictable that they're no fun anymore. This one has the kick of fresh ginger and powdered mustard to make it way out of the ordinary. Even the Ginger Cream Cheese Frosting is unusual if you follow our advice and flavor it with ginger wine and decorate the top with chopped crystallized ginger.

4 large eggs, at room temperature	½ teaspoon powdered mustard
2 cups granulated sugar	½ teaspoon freshly grated nutmeg
1½ cups canola or corn oil	1 cup chopped pecans or walnuts
2 cups all-purpose flour, sifted	½ cup currants
2 teaspoons baking soda	2 cups peeled and grated carrots
½ teaspoon salt	Ginger Cream Cheese Frosting
2 teaspoons cinnamon	(page 27) or confectioners' sugar
2 tablespoons minced peeled fresh	(optional)
gingerroot	

Preheat the oven to 350°F.

Butter a 12-inch round cake pan.

In the large bowl of an electric mixer set on medium speed, beat the eggs into the sugar one at a time, incorporating each one thoroughly before adding the next. Beat the oil into the egg mixture, then add the flour, baking soda, salt, cinnamon, ginger, mustard, and nutmeg, beating until all the ingredients are well mixed.

With a spatula or with the mixer set on low speed, fold in the nuts, currants, and grated carrots until well combined.

Pour the batter into the prepared cake pan and bake in the center of the oven for 1 hour and 20 minutes. Remove the cake from the oven and let cool in the pan on a wire rack. When cooled, invert the cake onto a large cake plate or platter and ice with the Ginger Cream Cheese Frosting, dust with confectioners' sugar, or serve plain.

HEART OF ARTICHOKE SPICE CAKE

Serves 8 to 12

*P*erhaps it's the baking soda that turns the artichokes in this cake a gorgeous forest green during the baking. The cake is maple-colored on the outside, but when cut into, the slices reveal the interior to be the deep, shimmery green of a rain forest. This moist, subtly spicy cake is an inspired ending to a St. Patrick's Day dinner or a Christmas feast. But don't save it for a special occasion. It's too good not to have often.

2	9-ounce packages frozen artichoke hearts, thawed	1	teaspoon baking powder
1	cup canola or corn oil	1	teaspoon cinnamon
1½	cups granulated sugar	½	teaspoon ground cloves
2	large eggs, at room temperature		Pinch of salt
2	cups all-purpose flour	1	cup chopped walnuts or pecans
1	teaspoon baking soda	1	cup raisins
			Confectioners' sugar for dusting

In a medium saucepan over high heat, bring 1 inch of water to a boil. Cook the artichoke hearts, uncovered, for 5 minutes; drain and puree in a food processor. Set aside.

Preheat the oven to 350°F.

Butter a 9-inch bundt pan.

In the large bowl of an electric mixer set at moderately high speed, beat the oil and sugar together until just combined. Add the eggs one at a time, beating well after each addition, and beat until creamy. Sift together the flour, baking soda, baking powder, cinnamon, cloves, and salt; add to the oil mixture and beat until smooth. Beat in the reserved artichoke puree until thoroughly blended. With a rubber spatula fold in the nuts and raisins. Transfer the batter to the bundt pan and bake in the center of the oven for 1 hour, or until a tester inserted in the middle of the cake comes out clean. Let cool in the pan on a wire rack for 10 to 15 minutes. Run a thin-bladed knife around the inner and outer edges of the bundt pan and invert onto a serving dish or cake stand. Dust with the confectioners' sugar.

Note ■ If you would like a higher, lighter-textured cake, separate the eggs, adding only the yolks to the oil and sugar, then beat the whites until they hold stiff peaks and fold them into the batter just before folding in the nuts and raisins.

PUMPKIN POUND CAKE WITH THREE LIQUEURS

Serves 10 to 16

*P*umpkin pound cake recipes often call for nuts in the batter, but nuts can overpower the delicate flavor of pumpkin. Instead, we add three flavored "brandies"—apricot, orange, and rum—to perfume the cake with a light and elusive fragrance. You may substitute peach brandy, which is more assertive, for the apricot.

3 cups sifted all-purpose flour

½ teaspoon salt

¼ teaspoon baking soda

1 cup (2 sticks) unsalted butter, softened

3 cups granulated sugar

6 large eggs, at room temperature

¾ cup homemade or canned pumpkin puree

¼ cup sour cream or low-fat yogurt

1 teaspoon pure vanilla extract

¼ cup apricot brandy

3 tablespoons orange liqueur (Cointreau, Triple Sec, or other)

3 tablespoons dark rum

Confectioners' sugar

Preheat the oven to 325°F.

Butter and flour a 2½-quart bundt pan.

In a medium bowl, sift the flour again with the salt and baking soda. Set aside.

In the large bowl of an electric mixer set on medium speed, cream the butter. Add the sugar about ½ cup at a time and beat the mixture until it is light and fluffy. Add the eggs one at a time, beating well after each addition. Beat in the pumpkin puree, sour cream, vanilla, apricot brandy, orange liqueur, and rum until thoroughly combined. Turn speed to medium-low and beat in the reserved flour mixture.

Pour the batter into the prepared bundt pan and bake the cake in the middle of the oven for 1 hour and 10 minutes, or until a cake tester inserted in the middle of the cake comes out clean. Let the cake cool in the pan on a wire rack for 1 hour, then turn it out onto the rack and let it cool completely. Dust with confectioners' sugar and transfer to a cake plate. Cut in thick wedges and serve.

Note ■ Try substituting ¼ cup of Frangelico (hazelnut liqueur) for the apricot brandy and 2 jiggers of cognac for the orange liqueur and rum.

AROMATIC SPICED PARSNIP BUNDT CAKE

Serves 10 to 12

*t*his cake has so much flavor and fragrance going for it that to frost or glaze it seems superfluous. A dusting of confectioners' sugar is all that's really necessary—and that only for aesthetic reasons. The flavor is complex, the texture is moist and chewy, and there's the additional bite of nuts and currants for your mouth to contend with. But if you must have a frosted cake, try our Brown Sugar Frosting.

4 large eggs, at room temperature	½ teaspoon dry mustard
2 cups granulated sugar	½ teaspoon freshly grated nutmeg
1½ cups canola or corn oil	1 cup chopped pecans or walnuts
2 cups all-purpose flour, sifted	½ cup currants
2 teaspoons baking soda	2 cups grated parsnips (about 1½
½ teaspoon salt	pounds, peeled)
2 teaspoons cinnamon	Confectioners' sugar for dusting
2 tablespoons peeled minced fresh	Brown Sugar Frosting (recipe
gingerroot	follows)

Preheat the oven to 350°F.

Butter a 9-inch bundt pan.

In the large bowl of an electric mixer set on medium speed, beat the eggs into the sugar one at a time, incorporating each one thoroughly before adding the next. Beat the oil into the egg mixture, then add the flour, baking soda, salt, cinnamon, gingerroot, mustard, and nutmeg, beating until well combined.

With a rubber spatula or with the electric mixer on low speed, fold in the nuts, currants, and grated parsnips until incorporated thoroughly.

Pour the batter into the prepared cake pan and bake in the center of the oven for 1 hour and 40 minutes, or until a tester inserted in the middle of the cake comes out clean. Remove from the oven and let cool in the pan on a wire rack for 10 to 15 minutes. Run a thin-bladed knife around the inner and outer edges of the bundt pan and invert onto a round serving platter or cake stand. Dust with confectioners' sugar or ice with Brown Sugar Frosting.

BROWN SUGAR FROSTING

½ cup firmly packed dark brown sugar

¼ cup heavy (whipping) cream

3 tablespoons unsalted butter, softened

7 tablespoons sifted confectioners' sugar

In a small saucepan over moderately high heat, whisk together the brown sugar, cream, and butter and bring to a boil. Cook, stirring constantly, for 2 minutes. Remove from the heat and whisk in the confectioners' sugar. Pour over the top of the cake and let any excess drip down the sides. This frosting will become firm and glossy as it cools.

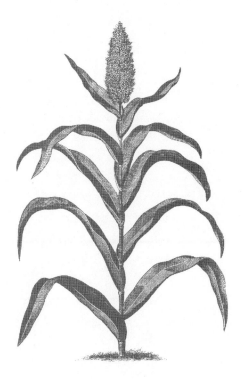

SWEET POTATO AND WALNUT COFFEE CAKE

Serves 8 to 12

$\mathcal{W}$e sometimes serve this loaf cake with dollops of cinnamon-sugar– or crystallized ginger–flavored whipped cream or ice cream, but mostly we serve it as is—plain and unadorned, moist and delicious.

CAKE

2 cups unsifted all-purpose flour

2 teaspoons baking powder

¼ teaspoon baking soda

½ teaspoon salt

1 teaspoon cinnamon

½ teaspoon freshly grated nutmeg

¼ teaspoon allspice

¼ teaspoon powdered ginger

½ cup chopped walnuts

4 tablespoons (½ stick) unsalted butter, melted and cooled

⅓ cup firmly packed light brown sugar

⅓ cup granulated sugar

3 large eggs, at room temperature

¼ cup sour cream

1 teaspoon pure vanilla extract

2 teaspoons finely grated orange zest

1 cup pureed cooked sweet potatoes, at room temperature

TOPPING

2 tablespoons cold unsalted butter, cut into small cubes

4 tablespoons chopped walnuts

3 tablespoons granulated sugar

1 teaspoon cinnamon

Preheat the oven to 350°F.

Lightly butter and flour a 9⅝ × 5½ × 2¾-inch loaf pan and set aside.

Sift together the flour, baking powder, baking soda, salt, cinnamon, nutmeg, allspice, and ginger. In a small bowl toss the walnuts with 1 teaspoon of the flour mixture (to keep the walnuts suspended in the batter during baking).

In the large bowl of an electric mixer set at medium speed, beat together the melted butter, brown sugar, and granulated sugar. Beat in the eggs one at a time, blending well after each addition. Beat in the sour cream, vanilla, orange rind, and pureed sweet potatoes. Add the sifted flour mixture and continue beating until combined well. With the electric mixer on the lowest speed, fold in the floured walnuts. Pour and scrape the batter into the prepared pan.

Crumble all the topping ingredients together in a small mixing bowl with your fingertips until the butter is in small bits. Sprinkle the topping evenly over the top and bake the cake in the lower third of the oven for about 45 minutes, or until a cake tester inserted into the center of the cake comes out clean and dry and the cake pulls slightly away from the sides of the pan. Let cool in the pan on a wire rack for 5 minutes. Invert onto the rack and invert again onto another rack to cool right side up.

SPICED ZUCCHINI TEA LOAVES

Makes 2 loaves

*O*ur sister-in-law, Barbara Stone, makes these legendary zucchini loaves in her Hamptons' kitchen to bring to friends as bread-and-butter gifts.

3 cups all-purpose flour	3 large eggs, at room temperature
1 teaspoon baking soda	2 cups granulated sugar
1 teaspoon salt	1 cup canola or vegetable oil
¼ teaspoon double-acting baking powder	1 tablespoon pure vanilla extract
3 teaspoons cinnamon	2 cups grated, unpeeled zucchini
1 teaspoon powdered ginger	1 cup coarsely chopped walnuts, pecans, or hazelnuts

Preheat the oven to 350°F.

Onto a large square of wax paper, sift together the flour, baking soda, salt, baking powder, cinnamon, and ginger. Set aside.

In the large bowl of an electric mixer set on medium speed, beat the eggs until light and foamy. Add the sugar and oil and continue beating until well combined. Add the vanilla and beat just until incorporated. Reduce the speed to medium-low and mix in the flour mixture until well blended. With the mixer or by hand, mix in the zucchini and the nuts until completely distributed. Divide the batter between two 8½ × 4½ × 2½-inch loaf pans and bake in the center of the oven for 1 hour, or until a tester comes out clean. Cool in the pans on wire racks for 5 minutes. Invert the loaves onto a plate, then invert again onto the racks to cool to room temperature. The loaves can be eaten as soon as they are cooled or wrapped in plastic wrap and left to develop even more flavor overnight. Securely wrapped, the loaves can be kept frozen up to 2 months.

MARBLED FENNEL COFFEE CAKE WITH SAMBUCA ESPRESSO GLAZE

Serves 8 or more

*M*arble cake is an American invention, but coffee beans in anise-flavored Sambuca liqueur or Sambuca splashed into a cup of espresso is an Italian inspiration. Combined in a cake, the two flavors make magic. We continue the synergy by topping it with a wildly exhilarating glaze. Is this a cake to have with coffee? Depends on how addicted you are. We like it with a glass of cold milk or hot chocolate.

¾ cup (1½ sticks) plus 1 tablespoon unsalted butter, softened

1 fennel bulb (about ¾ pound), washed, trimmed, and chopped fine or grated in a food processor plus 2 tablespoons minced green, feathery fronds

1 teaspoon fennel seeds

1 cup plus 2 tablespoons granulated sugar

1 tablespoon Sambuca, Pernod, anisette, or other licorice-flavored liqueur

2 cups sifted all-purpose flour

1 teaspoon baking powder

½ teaspoon baking soda

¼ teaspoon salt

2 large eggs

1 cup plain yogurt or sour cream

2 tablespoons instant espresso powder dissolved in 1 tablespoon hot water

Sambuca Espresso Glaze (recipe follows)

In a medium saucepan or skillet over moderate heat, melt 1 tablespoon of the butter and when the foam subsides, add the fennel and cook, stirring occasionally, for about 5 minutes, or until the fennel begins to soften. Stir in the minced fronds, fennel seeds, 2 tablespoons of the sugar, and the Sambuca and cook, stirring, until the sugar is completely dissolved. Reduce the heat to a simmer and continue cooking, stirring occasionally, for 10 minutes more, or until the fennel is very soft. Set aside to cool completely.

Preheat the oven to 350°F.

Butter an 8-inch (1½-quart) bundt pan well and set aside.

Sift together the flour, baking powder, baking soda, and salt onto a square of wax paper. In the bowl of an electric mixer, cream the butter on medium speed. Add the sugar gradually, beating the mixture until it is well combined and light and fluffy. Add the eggs one at a time, beating well after each addition. Add the flour mixture alternately with the yogurt, beginning and ending with the flour mixture, and blending the batter well after each addition. Transfer about one-third of the batter to a small bowl and stir in the espresso mixture until it is well combined. Stir the reserved fennel into the remaining batter until it is well combined. Spoon half the fennel batter into the prepared pan, spreading it evenly. Spoon all the coffee batter over it, spreading it evenly, then spoon the remaining fennel batter over that, spreading it evenly.

Bake the cake in the center of the oven for 60 to 65 minutes, or until it is golden and a tester comes out clean. Transfer the cake in the pan to a rack to cool for 30 minutes, then invert it onto the rack and let it cool completely before pouring the glaze over the cake and transferring it to a footed cake stand or serving platter. Cut in wedges and serve.

Note ■ We sometimes reserve some of the fennel fronds for garnishing the serving platter. Dampen short, well-formed fronds with water, shake dry, and dip them in granulated sugar, making sure it adheres, and place these sugar-gilded fronds around the base of the cake. Of course, save any fennel trimmings for soup or vegetable stock.

This cake also takes well to a heavy dusting of cinnamon sugar (taking its flavor cue again from the Italian: the sprinkling of cinnamon on cappuccino).

This recipe can be doubled and baked in a 10-inch (2½-quart) bundt pan for 10 to 15 minutes longer, or until a tester comes out clean.

SAMBUCA ESPRESSO GLAZE

2 tablespoons strong brewed coffee	1½ teaspoons instant espresso powder
1 tablespoon Sambuca, Pernod, anisette, or other licorice-flavored liqueur	¾ cup confectioners' sugar

Stir together the brewed coffee, Sambuca, and the espresso powder in a bowl until the powder is dissolved. Sift the confectioners' sugar and stir into the glaze until it is well combined. It should be of pourable consistency; if not, add more brewed coffee or Sambuca, but not more than 1 tablespoon. Pour the glaze carefully over the cake, letting it drip down the sides. Let the cake stand for 10 minutes, or until the glaze is set before transferring it to a footed cake stand or platter.

BASIC CHICKPEA FLOURLESS CAKE

Serves 6 to 8

*t*his is the cake that started it all. We adapted this recipe from one we discovered in an old Mexican cookbook. The original called for soaking the dried beans overnight and cooking them in salted water. (Never *ever* cook beans in salted water: the salt retards absorption of water and the beans will not tenderize.) Canned beans work just fine if they are drained and rinsed well under cold running water. The puree is then mixed with eggs, sugar, baking powder, and flavoring—no shortening, no butter—for a dense-textured, moist, chewy cake. It's wonderful with just a dusting of confectioners' sugar, but it can be served with ice cream, fresh fruit, preserves, or whipped cream. We call this a "basic" recipe because it allows for all kinds of variations and inventions. We even use it as the base for the newly styled and fennel-flavored Tiramisu on page 130.

2 cups canned chickpeas, drained	Grated zest of 1 lemon
4 eggs, at room temperature	Juice of 1 lemon
1 cup granulated sugar	Confectioners' sugar for dusting
½ teaspoon baking powder	

Preheat the oven to 350°F.

Butter or oil a 9-inch cake pan, cut a round of wax paper to fit the bottom, set in place, and butter or oil the paper.

Rinse the chickpeas well and drain. Discard any loose skins. Puree the drained chickpeas in a food processor until very smooth. Add the eggs, sugar, baking powder, and lemon zest and pulse a few times to blend all the ingredients completely, scraping down the sides and pulsing again, if necessary.

Pour and scrape the batter into the prepared pan and bake in the center of the oven for 45 minutes, or until a tester inserted in the center comes out clean.

Invert onto a rack to cool for 15 minutes, lift the pan from the cake, and remove the paper. While still warm or just before serving, drizzle the lemon juice over the cake and dust generously with the confectioners' sugar. Transfer to a serving platter.

Note ■ For a flavor variation, substitute 2 or 3 tablespoons orange zest for the lemon zest and ¼ cup of orange juice for the lemon juice. Sift together 2 tablespoons unsweetened cocoa powder with ½ cup confectioners' sugar and dust the cake with the mixture.

SPICY PINTO BEAN FRUIT AND NUT CAKE

Serves 10

*f*ruit cakes are usually made with a combination of dried fruits, glacéed fruits, candied orange peel, and nuts all soaked in spirits and aged. We're impatient. Save those dense dark fruitcakes for Christmas and serve this one all year long. It's more cakelike, fresher tasting, and infinitely lighter. And, not detracting from its appeal, a lot more healthy. Although made with beans, it also contains flour, so it's not to be offered to anyone who is allergic to grains.

2 cups pinto bean puree, made from unseasoned home-cooked or canned beans (rinsed and drained)

1 large egg, lightly beaten

4 tablespoons (½ stick) unsalted butter, melted

1 cup granulated sugar

1 cup all-purpose flour

1 teaspoon baking soda

¼ teaspoon salt

1 teaspoon cinnamon

1 teaspoon allspice

½ teaspoon ground cloves

2 cups cored, peeled, and chopped Greening, McIntosh, or Granny Smith apples

½ cup chopped walnuts

½ cup currants

½ cup golden raisins

2 teaspoons pure vanilla extract

Confectioners' sugar for dusting

10 walnut halves for decoration

Preheat the oven to 375°F.

Generously butter a 10-inch tube pan.

In the bowl of a food processor, puree the beans with the egg and melted butter. Add the sugar, flour, baking soda, salt, cinnamon, allspice, and cloves and pulse until well combined. Scrape the batter into a mixing bowl and with a spatula stir in the apples, walnuts, currants, raisins, and vanilla. Stir until thoroughly blended.

Scrape and pour the batter into the prepared tube pan and bake in the center of the oven for 1 hour, or until a tester inserted into the cake comes out clean. Invert onto a rack, remove the pan, and let cool completely. Dust with confectioners' sugar and decorate with the walnut halves.

ORANGE CREAM GARBANZO BEAN LAYER CAKE

Serves 8

a cake made with bean puree is moist enough, but a cake that is soaked in orange syrup, has custard between the layers, and is frosted with more custard mixed with whipped cream becomes puddinglike—an upright version of the Italian dessert, zuppa inglese, which is their take on English trifle. This all sounds very confusing but don't let that stop you from enjoying this wet, rich, citrusy cake. It's appropriate after a casual meal, a more elegant one, or just as a reward, anytime.

1 recipe Basic Chickpea Flourless Cake (page 20)

ORANGE SYRUP

⅓ cup granulated sugar

3 tablespoons grated orange zest

⅓ cup water

2 tablespoons Cointreau, Triple Sec, or Grand Marnier

ORANGE CUSTARD

2¼ cups milk

1 4-inch vanilla bean

5 large egg yolks

½ cup granulated sugar

3 tablespoons cornstarch

2 tablespoons grated orange zest

1 tablespoon fresh orange juice

½ cup very cold heavy (whipping) cream

Bake the cake and set it aside to cool while you make the syrup. In a small saucepan over moderate heat, combine the sugar, orange zest, water, and orange liqueur and bring to a boil, stirring. Reduce heat to a simmer and cook for 5 minutes. Set aside to cool, then strain through a sieve, pressing hard on the zest to extract any liquid. Scrape the zest from the sieve and reserve in a bowl for use as decoration after the cake is frosted.

To make the custard, in a small saucepan over moderately high heat, scald the milk with the vanilla bean. Discard the vanilla bean or save for another use. In a medium bowl whisk the yolks well, then whisk in the sugar and cornstarch. Add the scalded milk in a slow stream, whisking, until well combined. Pour the milk mixture back into the saucepan set over moderate heat and cook, stirring, until the mixture thickens. Reduce heat to a simmer and continue to cook, stirring occasionally, for 10 minutes. Add the orange zest and juice and stir until completely blended. Let cool, covered with a round of wax paper, then chill for 1 hour.

To assemble the cake, slice it horizontally into 2 layers. Brush the cut sides generously with the syrup. Set the bottom layer on a serving platter, cut side up, and spread with ¾ cup of the custard. Set the second layer, cut side down, on the custard. In the chilled bowl of an electric mixer or with a hand mixer at medium speed, beat the cream until it holds stiff peaks. With a rubber spatula fold it into the remaining custard and spread the top and sides of the cake with this cream mixture. Decorate the edge of the cake with the reserved orange zest. Cover lightly and chill for at least 2 hours or overnight before serving.

Note ■ We have made this cake very successfully using lemon zest and lemon juice instead of orange. Grapefruit and tangerine are other unusual flavors to try (if you do use tangerine, substitute tangerine liqueur, if you have it, for the orange liqueur in the syrup). Another idea which works wonderfully well is to substitute the pulp of a small ripe mango for the orange zest and juice in the custard.

RED BEAN DEVIL'S FOOD CAKE WITH COCOA-CREAM ICING

Serves 8

*Y*et another chocolate cake? Can there be too many? This one is different, however, moister because of the beans and very chocolaty tasting, dark and rich under a mantle of smooth brown velvet.

2 ounces (2 squares) unsweetened chocolate

3 cups red kidney bean puree, made from home-cooked or canned beans (rinsed and drained)

1 teaspoon baking powder

½ teaspoon baking soda

½ teaspoon salt

3 large eggs, lightly beaten

1½ cups granulated sugar

2 tablespoons Dutch-process cocoa

1 teaspoon instant espresso powder

¾ cup vegetable oil

½ cup chopped walnuts

1 recipe Cocoa-Cream Icing (recipe follows)

Preheat the oven to 350° F.

Line 2 buttered 8-inch cake pans with wax paper, butter the wax paper, and dust lightly with flour, knocking out the excess.

In a small heavy saucepan over the lowest possible heat or in the top of a double boiler over simmering water, melt the chocolate. Let cool slightly.

In a food processor combine the bean puree, baking powder, baking soda, salt, eggs, and melted chocolate and process until well blended. Add the sugar, cocoa, espresso powder, and oil and pulse several times until well combined. Add the walnuts and pulse once or twice or until just distributed.

Divide the batter between the two pans and bake the layers side by side in the center of the oven for 45 minutes, or until a tester inserted in the center comes out clean. Set pans on racks to cool for 15 minutes, then invert on racks, remove the pans, and strip off the wax paper. Let the layers cool completely.

To assemble the cake, place one layer of the cake, bottom side up, on a cake plate and with a metal spatula spread it with one-third of the Cocoa-Cream Icing. Place the second layer, bottom side down, over it and spread the top and sides with the remaining icing. Chill the cake for at least an hour or overnight. Remove from the refrigerator at least ½ hour before serving.

Note ■ The top and/or sides of the cake can be adorned with chocolate bits, chopped nuts, raisins, currants, dried apricot halves, a pile of julienned orange zest cooked in sugar syrup and drained, chocolate coffee beans, fresh strawberries, sugared snow pea pods, or dozens of other decorations, none of which are really necessary but do make a more festive-looking cake to serve to company or at a children's party.

COCOA-CREAM ICING

1 8-ounce package cream cheese, softened

½ cup (1 stick) unsalted butter, softened

1 pound confectioners' sugar, sifted

1 tablespoon coffee-flavored liqueur, such as Kahlúa or 1 teaspoon vanilla extract

⅔ cup Dutch-process cocoa powder

In the large bowl of an electric mixer set on medium speed, beat together the cream cheese and butter until the mixture is smooth. Beat in the confectioners' sugar in four batches until completely incorporated. Beat in the coffee liqueur and cocoa.

FRESH TOMATO DATE AND NUT SPICE CAKE WITH VANILLA CREAM CHEESE FROSTING

Serves 10 to 12

*t*his cake uses *fresh* tomatoes. Fresh, in this case, means the vine-ripened tomatoes available only during the tomato season—whenever that is, wherever you live. Out of season, choose another cake to make.

3 cups all-purpose flour	2 large eggs, at room temperature
2 teaspoons baking powder	½ cup chopped walnuts
1 teaspoon baking soda	½ cup chopped dates
1 teaspoon powdered ginger	½ cup golden raisins
½ teaspoon freshly grated nutmeg	2 cups peeled, seeded, and cubed
½ teaspoon salt	tomatoes
1 cup firmly packed dark brown sugar	Vanilla Cream Cheese Frosting
½ cup solid shortening	(recipe follows)

Preheat the oven to 350°F.

Grease and flour a 9 × 13 × 2-inch baking pan.

On a large sheet of wax paper, sift together the flour, baking powder, baking soda, ginger, nutmeg, and salt. Set aside.

In the large bowl of an electric mixer set on medium speed, cream together the sugar and the shortening until light and fluffy. Add the eggs, walnuts, dates, raisins, and tomatoes and continue to beat until well combined. Still beating, add the reserved flour mixture gradually and beat until completely blended. Pour into the prepared pan and bake in the center of the oven for 30 minutes. Cool in the pan on a wire rack. When completely cool, frost with Vanilla Cream Cheese Frosting, cut in squares, and arrange on a serving platter or footed cake stand.

VANILLA CREAM CHEESE FROSTING

1 8-ounce package cream cheese, softened	3 tablespoons unsalted butter, softened
1½ cups confectioners' sugar	⅛ teaspoon salt
2 teaspoons pure vanilla extract	

In the large bowl of an electric mixer set on moderately high speed, beat together the cream cheese, sugar, vanilla, butter, and salt until smooth.

Variation ■ For Ginger Cream Cheese Frosting, reduce the vanilla to 1 teaspoon and add 2 tablespoons finely chopped crystallized ginger.

CANNELLINI CLOUD CAKE

Serves 8

Similar to an angel food cake (it has an airy, spongy texture), this is the perfect, low-cholesterol ending to any meal. We often add a cup of raisins or currants, glacéed fruits, or nuts to the batter just to jazz it up a bit.

2 cups canned cannellini beans, drained

½ cup evaporated milk

4 large eggs, separated, at room temperature

½ teaspoon baking powder

1 cup plus 2 tablespoons granulated sugar

Grated zest of 1 lemon

Juice of 1 lemon

Confectioners' sugar for dusting

Preheat the oven to 350°F.

Butter or oil an angel food cake pan and set aside.

Rinse the cannellini beans under running water, drain well, and discard any loose skins. Place the beans and evaporated milk in a food processor and puree by pulsing several times until very smooth. Add the egg yolks, baking powder, 1 cup sugar, and lemon zest to the puree and pulse several times to blend all the ingredients thoroughly, scraping down the sides and pulsing again, if necessary.

With an electric mixer or hand mixer set on moderately high speed, beat the egg whites until soft peaks form. Add the remaining sugar and beat until stiff peaks form. With a rubber spatula fold the batter gently but thoroughly into the meringue. Pour and scrape the batter into the prepared pan and bake in the center of the oven for 1 hour and 10 minutes, or until a tester inserted into the center of the cake comes out clean. Cool completely on a rack. Before serving, drizzle the lemon juice over the cake and sprinkle generously with confectioners' sugar.

TOMATO SURPRISE FOUR-LAYER CAKE WITH COCONUT SOUR CREAM FROSTING

Serves 10 to 12

*t*his is a cake for an occasion—a skyscraper, a showstopper. But that's not all: it's moist, it's rich, it's dense, it's delicious. It combines the tartness of tomatoes with the sweet chewiness of coconut, then adds the citrus complexity of lemon and orange zest and the smoothness of sour cream. Try serving it at a dessert buffet. It's an impressive contender that can hold its own against any competition.

½ cup (1 stick) unsalted butter or margarine, softened

1½ cups granulated sugar

2 large eggs, at room temperature

2¼ cups all-purpose flour

1 tablespoon grated lemon zest

4 teaspoons baking powder

1 teaspoon baking soda

½ teaspoon salt

½ cup milk

3 large ripe tomatoes (about 1¼ pounds), peeled, seeded, chopped, and drained well (about 2 cups)

Coconut Sour Cream Frosting (recipe follows)

Preheat the oven to 350°F.

Butter two 9-inch round cake pans.

In the large bowl of an electric mixer on medium speed, beat together the butter, sugar, eggs, flour, lemon zest, baking powder, baking soda, salt, and milk for about 3 minutes, or until well blended. With a rubber spatula, fold in the tomatoes. Pour the batter into the pans and bake in the center of the oven for 25 to 30 minutes, or until a cake tester inserted in the center comes out clean. Cool in the pans on wire racks for 10 minutes, then turn the layers out on racks to cool them completely.

Using a sharp, serrated knife, carefully cut each layer horizontally in two. Place one layer, cut side up, on a cake platter and spread with one-fourth the Coconut Sour Cream Frosting. Repeat with the remaining layers and frosting, ending with frosting on top of the cake. Do not spread frosting over the sides. Sprinkle the top with the toasted coconut and serve. If making ahead and chilling, remove the cake from the refrigerator at least ½ hour before serving.

COCONUT SOUR CREAM FROSTING

2 7-ounce packages sweetened
   coconut flakes (about 5 cups)
1 cup confectioners' sugar

1 tablespoon grated orange zest
2 cups sour cream

Preheat the oven to 350°F.

Spread ¼ cup coconut on a baking sheet and toast in the oven until just golden brown. Set aside for decoration. In a large bowl combine the remaining coconut, confectioners' sugar, and grated orange zest. Stir in the sour cream and mix until well blended.

GINGERY FRESH GINGERROOT GINGERBREAD

Serves 8 to 10

*M*ost gingerbreads use only ground ginger for the ginger flavoring. We use both fresh and ground so the ginger taste overpowers the molasses and not vice versa. You may consider the addition of dry mustard odd, but it was part of early colonial gingerbread recipes. We usually serve this gingerbread warm with a mound of sweetened whipped cream, vanilla ice cream, or frozen yogurt as an added attraction.

2½ cups all-purpose flour

1½ teaspoons baking soda

½ teaspoon baking powder

1 teaspoon cinnamon

1 teaspoon powdered ginger

½ teaspoon ground cloves

2 teaspoons dry mustard

½ cup (1 stick) unsalted butter, softened

½ cup granulated sugar

1 large egg, at room temperature

1 cup unsulfured molasses

½ cup finely grated peeled fresh gingerroot

1 cup hot water

Preheat the oven to 350°F.

Generously butter a 9 × 9 × 2-inch baking pan. Set aside.

On a large sheet of wax paper, sift together the flour, baking soda, baking powder, cinnamon, powdered ginger, cloves, and mustard. Set aside.

In the large bowl of an electric mixer set on moderately high speed, cream together the butter and sugar until light and fluffy. Reduce the speed to medium and beat in the egg and molasses for 1 minute, or until well combined. Add the fresh ginger and continue beating until it is completely incorporated. Reduce the speed to moderately low and beat in the flour mixture alternately with the hot water in four batches, ending with the flour mixture. When completely mixed together, increase the speed to high and beat for 30 seconds more, or until very smooth. Pour the batter into the prepared baking pan and bake for 45 to 50 minutes. Cool in the pan on a wire rack for 10 minutes. Invert the gingerbread onto the wire rack and let cool briefly. Serve in squares or rectangles. Of course, the gingerbread can be served at room temperature as well.

Note ■ If you like the crunch of nuts, add ½ cup of your favorite kind (broken in small pieces and dusted with flour) to the batter before pouring it into the baking pan.

CREAM CHEESE-CHICKPEA-HAZELNUT POUND CAKE

Serves 8

*M*ace is the indefinable flavoring that distinguishes traditional pound cakes from others. We make this one without flour, substituting pureed chickpeas in its place. We also add cream cheese and hazelnuts so our pound cake is anything but traditional—except for the mace. It's also exceptionally moist. For a nutless cake, substitute chopped prunes, dried apricots, currants, or raisins instead.

1 8-ounce package cream cheese, softened

¾ cup (1½ sticks) unsalted butter, softened

1¾ cups granulated sugar

1½ teaspoons pure vanilla extract

5 large eggs, at room temperature

2 cups chickpea puree, made from unseasoned home-cooked or canned chickpeas (rinsed and drained)

½ teaspoon mace, or more to taste

1½ teaspoons baking powder

1 cup chopped toasted hazelnuts (see Note)

Confectioners' sugar for dusting

Preheat the oven to 350°F.

Butter and flour a 10 × 4½-inch tube pan with a removable bottom or a bundt pan.

In the bowl of an electric mixer, beat the cream cheese and the butter until the mixture is light and creamy. Continue beating and add the sugar a little at a time until well combined. Add the vanilla, then the eggs one at a time, beating well after each addition. Add the chickpea puree, mace, and baking powder and beat until just combined. Stir the hazelnuts into the mixture and pour the batter into the prepared pan. Bake in the middle of the oven for 1 hour and 50 minutes to 2 hours, or until a cake tester inserted in the center comes out clean. Let the cake cool in the pan on a rack for 10 minutes, then invert it onto the rack and let it cool in the pan completely. Remove the pan and sift the confectioners' sugar over the cake.

Note ■ To toast whole hazelnuts, preheat the oven to 350°F. Spread the hazelnuts in one layer on a baking pan and toast for 10 to 15 minutes. Wrap the nuts in a dishtowel and let them steam for 1 minute. Rub them in the towel to remove the skins and cool.

DOUBLE DEMON GINGER POUND CAKE

Serves 10 to 14

*t*oo often the only ginger in ginger-flavored recipes is powdered ginger, a somewhat bland spice, and even then it's disguised by mixing it with more powerful flavorings like cinnamon and cloves. We try to use fresh or crystallized ginger or both when we want the flavor and zippiness of the *real* thing. Certainly, you couldn't mistake the flavor of this cake for anything but—it packs a mighty punch. All this and a crunchy crust and moist cake, too! Heavenly, but hot as hell.

1 cup (2 sticks) unsalted butter, softened	½ teaspoon salt
	½ cup buttermilk
2 cups granulated sugar	2 tablespoons grated peeled fresh gingerroot
4 large eggs, at room temperature	
2½ cups all-purpose flour	1 cup coarsely chopped crystallized ginger
1 teaspoon baking powder	
½ teaspoon baking soda	

Preheat the oven to 350°F.

Butter a 3-quart bundt pan or other decorative tube pan and dust with flour.

In the large bowl of an electric mixer set at medium speed, cream the butter. Add the sugar a little at a time, and continue beating until the mixture is light and fluffy. Add the eggs one at a time, beating to combine well after each addition.

Onto a sheet of wax paper, sift together the flour, baking powder, baking soda, and salt. Add the flour mixture to the butter mixture alternately with the buttermilk in three batches, beginning and ending with the flour mixture. Beat the batter after each addition to combine. Reduce speed to low and fold in the grated gingerroot and crystallized ginger until thoroughly distributed.

With a rubber spatula, spoon and scrape the batter into the prepared pan and bake in the center of the oven for 1 hour and 20 minutes, or until a tester inserted midway between the sides of the pan comes out clean. Let the cake cool on a wire rack for 10 minutes, then invert onto the rack, remove the pan, and cool completely before serving.

Note ■ If well wrapped and kept in a cool, dry place or a cake tin with a tight-fitting lid, this cake will keep for more than a week. It can be kept frozen for 2 months.

CARROT AND BANANA COFFEE CAKE

Serves 8

*C*arrots and bananas, although from different parts of the world, marry well. Cut this in nice, inch-thick slices to serve with tea—or for breakfast with coffee.

1 cup peeled and shredded carrot

2 cups all-purpose flour

1 teaspoon baking powder

¼ teaspoon baking soda

¼ teaspoon salt

1 tablespoon unsweetened cocoa powder

½ teaspoon cinnamon

¼ cup chopped pecans

½ cup (1 stick) unsalted butter, softened

¾ cup firmly packed brown sugar

1 extra-large egg, at room temperature

2 extra-large egg yolks, at room temperature

1 teaspoon pure vanilla extract

1½ cups mashed ripe bananas

Preheat the oven to 350°F.

Lightly butter and flour a 9 × 5 × 3-inch loaf pan and set aside.

Spread ½ cup of the shredded carrot on a small baking sheet and place in the oven for 4 or 5 minutes. The carrot should become dry and fragrant. Cool completely.

Sift together the flour, baking powder, baking soda, salt, cocoa, and cinnamon. In a small bowl, toss the pecans with ½ teaspoon sifted flour mixture.

In the large bowl of an electric mixer set on moderately high speed, cream the butter for 2 or 3 minutes. Add the brown sugar and continue beating for 1 to 2 minutes more, or until light and fluffy and well combined. Beat in the egg, the egg yolks, and the vanilla. Add the mashed bananas and blend together. Turn the speed to low and add the sifted flour in two batches, beating just until the flour has been absorbed into the mixture. By hand with a rubber spatula, fold in the pecans and the remaining ½ cup of shredded carrot. Pour and scrape the batter into the prepared pan. Sprinkle the top of the batter with the toasted carrot.

Bake the cake in the lower third of the oven for 50 to 55 minutes, or until well risen and a cake tester inserted into the center of the cake comes out clean and dry. The cake will pull away slightly from the sides of the pan when done.

Let cool in the pan on a wire rack for 5 minutes, then invert the cake onto the rack and remove the pan. Invert again onto another rack and cool right side up.

FRESH GINGER ANGEL FOOD CAKE WITH GINGERED BITTERSWEET CHOCOLATE FROSTING

Serves 10 to 12

*a*ngel food cakes made from egg whites—no yolks—and without butter are perfect for anyone on a low-fat, low-cholesterol diet. Certainly, there are calories, but they are not derived from fat. In this recipe the only butter is a tablespoon in the frosting. The cup of chocolate bits in the frosting contains cholesterol as well. So if you are cutting down on or cutting out fats altogether, don't ice this cake. Serve it instead with fresh or stewed peaches or pears, both of which are enhanced by the flavor of ginger, or dusted with confectioners' sugar, or sprinkled liberally with Stone's Ginger Wine (no relation, available at most liquor stores), or with a good-quality chocolate-flavored no-fat frozen yogurt.

4 ounces fresh gingerroot (about a 4-inch piece), peeled and coarsely chopped

1½ cups granulated sugar

1 cup cake flour

12 large egg whites, at room temperature

1½ teaspoons cream of tartar

¼ teaspoon salt

Gingered Bittersweet Chocolate Frosting (recipe follows)

Preheat the oven to 375°F.

In a food processor, combine the gingerroot and ¼ cup sugar and process, pulsing, until blended into a thick paste. Set aside.

On a sheet of wax paper, sift the flour and ¾ cup sugar together three times.

In the large bowl of an electric mixer set on high speed, beat the egg whites until foamy, about 1 minute. Add the cream of tartar and salt, and beat in the remaining ½ cup sugar a little at a time, beating constantly, until soft peaks form and hold their shape, about 5 minutes. Reduce the mixer speed to low and sprinkle the flour-sugar mixture over the meringue, ¼ cup at a time, folding in gently just until the flour-sugar mixture is incorporated. Still on low speed, add the reserved ginger paste and blend in. Do not overmix. Remove the bowl from the mixer and, with a rubber spatula, fold a few times to ensure the paste is well combined. Transfer the batter to an ungreased 10-inch tube pan, running the spatula through the center of the batter to eliminate air pockets. Bake for 45 minutes, or until a cake tester inserted in the center of the cake midway between the two edges of the pan comes out clean. Invert the pan on a wire rack and let cool completely before running a knife around the sides of the cake and inverting it onto a cake platter or cake stand. Using a metal spatula, smooth Gingered Bittersweet Chocolate Frosting over the top and sides of the cake.

GINGERED BITTERSWEET CHOCOLATE FROSTING

1 cup semisweet chocolate bits

1 tablespoon unsalted butter

⅓ cup very strong coffee

1 cup confectioners' sugar

2 tablespoons finely minced
   crystallized ginger

In a small saucepan over the lowest possible heat, melt the chocolate bits, butter, and coffee together, stirring occasionally. Cool to lukewarm and stir in the sugar and crystallized ginger. Beat with a whisk until thick enough to spread. This recipe makes enough frosting to cover the cake completely and generously.

BEET-APPLE-GINGER
UPSIDE-DOWN CAKE

Serves 8

*f*resh beets are so sweet that it seems odd to us that cooks use them only for soups, stews, pickles, and as a side dish. In some countries only the leaves are cooked, and the roots are relegated to farm animals as fodder. Of course, some beets are grown for their sugar content alone and so find a back door into our dessert repertoire, albeit incognito, offering neither original color nor flavor to a recipe. This cake partners tart apples with zingy ginger and offers beets for sweetness and the shock of color.

TOPPING

2 tablespoons unsalted butter, melted

¼ cup granulated sugar

½ teaspoon powdered ginger

¼ teaspoon cinnamon

1 large, tart cooking apple, such as Granny Smith, sliced ¼ inch thick and tossed with 1 tablespoon lemon juice

1 large fresh beet (preferably equal in size to the apple), peeled and sliced ¼ inch thick

¼ cup finely chopped crystallized ginger

CAKE

1⅓ cups all-purpose flour

¾ teaspoon double-acting baking powder

¼ teaspoon salt

¼ teaspoon freshly grated nutmeg

¼ teaspoon cinnamon

¼ teaspoon ground cloves

3 tablespoons solid shortening or margarine

1 tablespoon unsalted butter, softened

¼ cup firmly packed light brown sugar

2 teaspoons pure vanilla extract

1 tablespoon minced fresh gingerroot or ½ teaspoon ground ginger

2 large eggs, at room temperature

½ cup maple syrup

½ cup plus 1 tablespoon milk, at room temperature

Preheat the oven to 350°F.

Lightly butter an 8-inch round baking pan, then pour the 2 tablespoons melted butter on the bottom of the pan, tipping to coat evenly.

Mix together the sugar, powdered ginger, and cinnamon and sprinkle evenly over the melted butter. Alternate the apple and beet slices over the sugar mixture, overlapping them closely in a spiral pattern. Sprinkle the chopped ginger on top and set aside.

Onto a large sheet of wax paper, sift the flour with the baking powder, salt, nutmeg, cinnamon, and cloves. In the large bowl of an electric mixer set on moderately high speed, cream the shortening and butter for 1 to 2 minutes, or until smooth and fluffy. Add the brown sugar, vanilla, and minced gingerroot and beat 1 minute longer, or until well combined. Set the mixer on low speed and beat in half the sifted flour, the eggs, maple syrup, and all of the milk, then beat in the remaining flour, beating 1 or 2 minutes more until thoroughly blended. Pour the batter carefully over the apple-beet-ginger mixture, trying not to disturb the arrangement.

Bake the cake in the lower third of the oven for 35 to 40 minutes, or until a cake tester inserted in the center comes out clean and the cake pulls slightly away from the sides of the pan.

Transfer the cake in its pan to a rack to cool for about 5 minutes. Run a thin, sharp knife around the inside of the pan to loosen the cake and invert onto a round serving platter.

Serve the cake warm or at room temperature cut into thick wedges.

Note ■ This cake can be glazed with currant jelly if you like a shinier, more even appearance. In a small saucepan over low heat, melt ⅓ cup red currant jelly, stirring, until liquefied. Brush it over the cake.

CARROT CAKE STUDDED WITH NUTS AND APRICOTS CLOAKED IN ORANGE GLAZE

Serves 10 to 12

*W*hen we first made this cake, it had raisins in it and was spread with a cream cheese frosting, just like all the other carrot cakes we ever had. Boring. Carrots are orange, oranges are orange, apricots are orange. Why not combine our love of three oranges in a cake, we reasoned. This is the result. Another change for the better: we've replaced half the white flour with whole wheat flour to make the cake nuttier tasting, the crust crustier.

2 cups granulated sugar	3 cups peeled and grated raw carrots
1¼ cups canola or corn oil	1 cup finely chopped walnuts dusted
1 cup sifted whole wheat flour	with just enough flour to coat
1 cup all-purpose flour	lightly (about a level teaspoon)
2 tablespoons baking powder	½ cup finely chopped dried apricots
1 teaspoon baking soda	dusted with just enough flour to
1 teaspoon salt	coat lightly (a scant teaspoon)
2 tablespoons cinnamon	Orange Glaze (recipe follows)
4 large eggs, at room temperature	

Preheat the oven to 350°F.

Oil a 10-inch tube pan and set aside.

In the large bowl of an electric mixer set at medium speed, thoroughly combine the sugar and the oil.

On a sheet of wax paper, sift together both flours, baking powder, baking soda, salt, and cinnamon. Add half the dry ingredients to the sugar-oil mixture and beat at medium speed until thoroughly combined, about 2 to 3 minutes. Beat in the remaining dry ingredients in four batches, alternating with the eggs added one at a time, beating well after each addition. Beat in the carrots, walnuts, and apricots until just combined.

Pour the batter into the prepared tube pan and bake in the center of the oven for 1 hour and 10 minutes, or until a cake tester inserted in the center of the cake midway between the two edges of the pan comes out clean. Remove the cake from the oven and let it cool in the pan in an upright position. While the cake is cooling, make the orange glaze. When both cake and glaze have cooled completely, run a thin knife between the cake and the edges of the pan and invert the cake onto a cake platter. Pour the Orange Glaze over the cake, spreading it with a metal spatula and letting it drip down the sides.

ORANGE GLAZE

1 cup granulated sugar	2 tablespoons unsalted butter
¼ cup cornstarch	2 tablespoons grated orange rind
1 cup freshly squeezed orange juice	¼ teaspoon salt
1 teaspoon freshly squeezed lemon juice	

In a small saucepan, mix together the sugar, cornstarch, and the two juices. When the mixture is well combined and smooth, set the saucepan over low heat and add the butter, orange rind, and salt. Cook the mixture, stirring constantly, until it is thick and glossy, about 3 minutes. Let the glaze cool completely before pouring over the cooled cake.

GÂTEAU TOPINAMBOUR, OR JERUSALEM ARTICHOKE CHOCOLATE CAKE

Serves 8 to 12

*J*erusalem artichokes are native to North America, although they are more popular in Europe than they are here. The French call them *topinambour,* thus the name of this cake. And that's about the only thing French about it. The cake is smooth textured and rich and keeps well if refrigerated (bring to room temperature before serving). If you've never tried Jerusalem artichokes (also called sunchokes), look for them in the late fall and throughout the winter. Northeastern and midwestern varieties are often left in the ground to winter and harvested in the spring after the sugars in the tubers have undergone a chemical change because of the cold weather. They are sweetest then and most digestible. For this recipe, scrub them well, cut them in small chunks, and boil or steam them with the skins on for about 15 minutes, or until they are very tender. Then drain and mash with a potato masher or puree them in a food processor or blender.

7½ ounces best-quality semisweet chocolate, chopped

¾ cup (1½ sticks) unsalted butter

4 large eggs, separated, at room temperature

½ cup plus 1 tablespoon granulated sugar

1 pound Jerusalem artichokes, cooked (see headnote for procedure) and pureed

¼ cup all-purpose flour

Confectioners' sugar for dusting

Sweetened whipped cream as accompaniment (optional)

Preheat the oven to 350°F.

Butter and flour a 10-inch round cake pan and line the bottom with a round of wax paper. Butter and flour the wax paper. Set aside.

In a small, heavy saucepan set over the lowest possible heat or in the top of a double boiler over barely simmering water, melt the chocolate and butter together. Stir and set aside to cool.

In the large bowl of an electric mixer set on medium speed, beat the egg yolks until light and fluffy. Still beating, add the sugar gradually, beating constantly until pale yellow. Turn the speed to low and fold in the chocolate and Jerusalem artichoke puree until just blended. Sift the flour over the chocolate mixture and beat on low speed until the flour is incorporated completely.

In another bowl, with a hand-held rotary or electric mixer set on high speed, beat the egg whites until soft peaks form. With a rubber spatula, fold half of the whites into the chocolate mixture gently but thoroughly. Add the rest of the whites and fold in gently just until no whites appear. Do not overmix.

Pour the batter into the prepared pan and spread it evenly with the rubber spatula. Tap the pan once or twice on a work surface to remove any air pockets. Bake in the center of the oven for 25 to 30 minutes, or until a cake tester inserted in the middle comes out with a few crumbs clinging to it. Set on a wire rack to cool in the pan for about 1 hour. Run a knife around the edge of the cake to loosen it and invert onto a cookie sheet. Peel off the wax paper and invert the cake again onto a serving platter. Sprinkle with confectioners' sugar and serve cut in wedges.

Note ■ We like to serve this cake with whipped cream sweetened with a nut-flavored liqueur (to emphasize the nutty taste of the Jerusalem artichokes) such as Amaretto or Frangelico but it's equally as good sweetened with a fruit- or vanilla-flavored liqueur. The cake will be very moist, almost puddinglike—and it should be. The Jerusalem artichokes will keep it that way for several days if stored, covered tightly, in the refrigerator.

BRANDIED CHOCOLATE CAKE WITH SUN-DRIED TOMATOES AND PECANS

Serves 8 to 12

Sun-dried tomatoes are a fairly recent addition to American pantries. Those used in this recipe are dry and sold loose or in cellophane bags, not preserved in oil. Their flavor and texture adds an unexpected complexity to the combination of chocolate, brandy, coffee, and nuts. This cake can feed more than its one layer would indicate; because it is so rich it should be offered in thin slices, each of its few bites to be relished. Actually, we should call it a torte because there is no flour in the recipe.

CAKE

½ cup chopped sun-dried tomatoes

¼ cup brandy, Armagnac, or kirsch

6 ounces German sweet chocolate or semisweet chocolate, coarsely chopped

3 tablespoons strong brewed coffee or espresso

½ cup (1 stick) unsalted butter, cut into bits and softened

3 large eggs, separated, at room temperature

½ cup plus 2 tablespoons granulated sugar

Pinch of salt

Pinch of cream of tartar

1 cup ground pecans

¼ cup cornstarch, sifted

FROSTING

4 ounces German sweet chocolate or semisweet chocolate, coarsely chopped

1 tablespoon brandy, Armagnac, or kirsch

3 tablespoons confectioners' sugar

4 tablespoons (½ stick) unsalted butter, cut into bits and softened

In a small, nonmetallic bowl let the sun-dried tomatoes soften in the brandy for 30 minutes.

Line an 8½-inch round cake pan, 2 inches deep, with wax paper and butter and flour the paper. Set aside.

Preheat the oven to 350°F.

In a small, heavy saucepan set over the lowest possible heat or in the top of a double boiler set over simmering water, melt the chocolate with the coffee. Remove the pan from the heat, and with a hand mixer or by hand, beat in the butter bit by bit, making sure that each piece is incorporated before adding the next. Set aside.

In a large bowl with the hand mixer or a whisk, beat the egg yolks until smooth. Add ½ cup sugar a little at a time and beat the mixture until it thickens and falls from the beater or whisks in a ribbon when either is lifted. In a bowl with the hand mixer or the whisk cleaned and dried, beat the egg whites with the salt until just frothy. Add the cream of tartar and continue beating until they hold soft peaks. Beat in the remaining 2 tablespoons sugar a little at a time until the whites hold stiff peaks.

Stir the chocolate mixture into the yolk mixture and add the pecans, sun-dried tomatoes with their brandy, and the cornstarch. Stir one-third of the whites into the chocolate mixture thoroughly, then gently fold in the remaining whites until there are no traces of them left in the batter. Spoon the batter into the prepared cake pan and bake in the middle of the oven for 40 minutes, or until a tester inserted 2 inches from the rim comes out clean. The center of the cake will stay moist.

Transfer the cake in its pan to a rack and cool completely. Invert the cake onto the rack and peel off the wax paper. Transfer the inverted cake to a serving plate. Chill in the refrigerator for 1 hour, or until well chilled.

Meanwhile, make the frosting. In a small, heavy saucepan set over the lowest possible heat or in the top of a double boiler set over simmering water, melt the chocolate with the brandy. Remove the pan from the heat and stir in the confectioners' sugar. Stir in the butter bit by bit, making sure each piece is incorporated before the next is added.

With a metal spatula, spread the sides and top of the cake with the frosting and chill the cake until the frosting is set. Let the cake come to room temperature before serving in thin slices.

Note ■ Because this cake is served in thin slices we suggest cutting the cake in half before cutting each serving, especially if you are using a wedge-shaped cake or pie cutter (recommended because the center of this cake is so moist it needs the support of a wide implement to transport it). If the cake were left in the round, the blades of these serving pieces would be too wide to lift the first narrow slice cleanly free of the cake.

SAUERKRAUT BUTTERMILK CHOCOLATE LAYER CAKE WITH WHITE-ON-WHITE ICING

Serves 12 to 16

*t*his is an American recipe that must have been developed in Pennsylvania Dutch country. It just has that feeling. The early German settlers there were creative in their kitchens—and frugal. If there was leftover sauerkraut or too much in the larder, we have no doubt that one of those inventive cooks in a moment of complete abandon— or pique—dared to add some to a chocolate cake. Amazingly, it worked. The cake was moist, fudgy, and had no hint of fermented cabbage in the taste or smell. You may have heard about this cake and thought it was a joke. It's not. It's a serious winner.

¾ cup sauerkraut, rinsed, drained, and finely chopped

1½ cups buttermilk

¾ cup (1½ sticks) unsalted butter or margarine, softened

1¾ cups light brown sugar, firmly packed

2 teaspoons pure vanilla extract

2 large eggs, at room temperature

¾ cup unsweetened cocoa powder

2¼ cups all-purpose flour

1½ teaspoons baking powder

1 teaspoon baking soda

¼ teaspoon salt

White-on-White Icing (recipe follows)

Preheat the oven to 350°F.

Butter two 8-inch square baking pans and line the bottoms with buttered wax paper.

In a bowl, combine the sauerkraut and buttermilk and set aside.

In the large bowl of an electric mixer set at medium speed, beat the butter, brown sugar, and vanilla until fluffy. Add the eggs and beat until combined. In a small bowl, mix together the cocoa, flour, baking powder, baking soda, and salt. Turn the mixer to low speed and beat the cocoa mixture and sauerkraut mixture alternately into the butter mixture, beating just until the ingredients are blended.

Pour the batter into the prepared pans and bake in the center of the oven for 25 to 30 minutes, or until a cake tester inserted into the center of the cakes comes out clean or the layers spring back when lightly pressed with a finger. Let the pans cool on wire racks for 10 minutes. Turn the layers out on wire racks, strip off the wax paper, and let cool completely.

Transfer one layer upside down to a cake plate. With a metal spatula, smooth one-third of the frosting over the layer and place the second layer, right side up, over it. Swirl the rest of the frosting over the top and sides. Decorate and serve in 2- or 3-inch squares. If you are making this cake ahead, refrigerate and decorate just before serving.

WHITE-ON-WHITE ICING

1½ cups heavy (whipping) cream
3 tablespoons granulated sugar
1 teaspoon pure vanilla extract

½ cup flaked coconut, or more to
   taste

In the large bowl of an electric mixer set at high speed, beat the cream, sugar, and vanilla until soft peaks form. Frost the cake as above and sprinkle the top and sides with the coconut flakes.

MOIST MASHED POTATO CHOCOLATE CAKE

Serves 8 to 10

*O*ne thing about making cakes with vegetables—they always turn out moist. Potatoes keep this cake extra moist and don't affect the dark chocolate flavor. The cake keeps much longer than a chocolate cake made with white flour, and it also offers better nutrition. Serve it with flavored whipped cream or berry puree if you wish.

5 ounces best-quality bittersweet
  chocolate

1 tablespoon instant espresso powder

2 tablespoons Amaretto (Italian
  almond-flavored liqueur)

½ cup (1 stick) unsalted butter

4 large eggs, separated, at room
  temperature

½ cup granulated sugar

1 cup unseasoned mashed potatoes

½ cup finely ground almonds

  Pinch of salt

  Confectioners' sugar

Preheat the oven to 350°F.

Grease an 8-inch springform pan and line the bottom with a round of wax paper.

In a small saucepan set over the lowest possible heat or in the top of a double boiler set over simmering water, melt the chocolate together with the espresso powder, Amaretto, and butter. Stir to combine and set aside to cool.

In the large bowl of an electric mixer set at medium speed, beat together the egg yolks and sugar for about 3 minutes, or until the mixture is thick, creamy, and pale yellow. Reduce the speed to low, pour in the cooled chocolate mixture, and continue beating until just blended, about 1 minute. Add the mashed potatoes and almonds and continue to beat on low speed until thoroughly combined.

In a separate bowl, beat the egg whites with a pinch of salt until stiff but not dry. With a rubber spatula, fold the whites gently but thoroughly into the chocolate batter. Pour the batter into the prepared pan and bake in the center of the oven for 35 minutes, or until the sides are firm; the cake will be soft in the center.

Remove from the oven and cool in the pan on a wire rack for 1 hour. Run a thin knife around the sides of the cake to release it, remove the sides of the pan, and let the cake cool completely. Invert the cake onto a cake plate or cake stand, remove the bottom of the pan, and peel off the wax paper. Sprinkle with confectioners' sugar.

SWEET AND FLAKY SWISS CHARD
PHYLLO ROLL WITH RAISINS AND PINE NUTS

Serves 8

a few years ago, in Nice, we were served this classic dessert in the form of a two-crust pie. It was delicious. But never ones to leave well enough alone, we rolled up this Provençal tradition in Greek phyllo dough, baked it on a cookie sheet, and served it in thick slices for a dessert that is part French, part Greek, and a little Austrian.

1 pound Swiss chard leaves (green or red)	2 large eggs, lightly beaten
1 cup golden raisins	5 frozen phyllo leaves, thawed
½ cup pine nuts (pignoli) or pistachios	2 tablespoons unsalted butter, melted
	Confectioners' sugar for dusting

Preheat the oven to 375°F.

Lightly grease a cookie sheet and set aside.

Trim the chard leaves of white stems and tough white center vein. Tear the leaves coarsely and chop fine in a food processor or by hand. In a medium bowl, combine the chopped chard with the raisins, pine nuts, and eggs. Set aside.

Thaw the frozen phyllo leaves to room temperature according to the directions on the package. On a large sheet of wax paper, place one sheet of phyllo dough and brush it lightly all over with some of the melted butter. Cover this with another sheet of dough and brush it with the butter. Repeat with three more phyllo sheets, making five in all. With a rubber spatula, turn out and shape the filling into an even mound along the long side of the stack of dough, about 2 inches from the bottom edge, leaving about 1 inch of dough at either short end. Fold the short ends in and, using the wax paper to lift the phyllo, roll it carefully around the chard filling, enclosing it completely. Using the wax paper as a sling, transfer the roll to the prepared cookie sheet, seam side down. Brush the top and the ends with the remaining butter and bake in the center of the oven for 50 minutes. Cool on the cookie sheet. Transfer with two large metal spatulas to a serving plate and sprinkle with the confectioners' sugar. Serve in 1½- to 2-inch slices.

Note ■ You can serve the roll warm with ice cream, frozen low-fat yogurt, or sweetened whipped cream. But it's healthier and, we feel, just as good served plain.

MEXICAN JALAPEÑO CHOCOLATE CREAM CAKE

Serves 6 to 8

*W*e have never encountered this cake in Mexico. It's the combination of ingredients that triggered its name: jalapeño peppers, Kahlúa (Mexican coffee liqueur), cinnamon, and chocolate. Jalapeños find their way into scores of Mexican *antojitos* (appetizers) and main dishes, but not into desserts, as far as we can determine. We decided to try the four flavorings together after a friend brought us brownies laced with jalapeños and we loved them. They make your tongue tingle a little with their heat, but otherwise you'll have a hard time pinpointing their flavor in this moist, almost puddinglike cake.

4 ounces best-quality semisweet chocolate

2 tablespoons Kahlúa (or other coffee-flavored liqueur)

½ cup (1 stick) unsalted butter, softened

¾ cup plus 1 tablespoon granulated sugar

3 large eggs, separated, at room temperature

1 teaspoon pure vanilla extract

¾ cup all-purpose flour

1 teaspoon cinnamon

½ cup finely ground blanched (skinless) almonds

2 medium jalapeño peppers, seeded, de-ribbed, and finely minced (wear rubber gloves)

Pinch of salt

Preheat the oven to 350°F.

Butter an 8-inch round cake pan, cut a round of wax paper to fit and line the bottom, and then butter the wax paper. Set aside.

In a small, heavy saucepan over the lowest possible heat, or in the top of a double boiler set over simmering water, melt the chocolate with the Kahlúa. Stir together until smooth and set aside to cool.

In the large bowl of an electric mixer set on medium speed, cream together the butter and ¾ cup sugar until thick and pale yellow. Still beating, add the egg yolks one at a time, beating well after each addition, until completely incorporated. Turn the speed to low and mix in the chocolate mixture until thoroughly combined. Blend in the vanilla.

Add the flour, cinnamon, almonds, and jalapeños and continue beating until combined well.

In a separate bowl, with a hand or electric mixer, beat the egg whites with a pinch of salt until they form soft peaks. Add the remaining tablespoon sugar and continue beating until stiff peaks are formed. With a rubber spatula, fold one-third of the egg whites into the chocolate batter until thoroughly combined. Then fold in the remaining egg whites gently and continue folding until no streaks of white are visible.

Pour the batter into the prepared pan and bake in the center of the oven for 25 minutes. The cake will seem quite soft and underbaked in the center. This is the way it is supposed to be. Let cool in the pan on a wire rack to room temperature or for at least ½ hour. Run a thin, sharp knife around the edge, invert the cake onto a cake plate or footed cake stand, and peel off the wax paper.

Note ■ This cake can be served plain, dusted with confectioners' sugar and each serving mounded with Kahlúa-flavored whipped cream.

ACORN SQUASH GINGER CREAM LOG

Serves 6 to 10

*t*his is one of our favorite desserts of all. It never ceases to bring dinner party conversation to a halt; oohs and ahs take over, speculation on ingredients, exclamations over the texture, the flavor, the lightness, the richness, pleas for the recipe. Oh dear! Talk of the theater, movies, politics, the environment, travel, news—it all ends. We have stopped serving it to any but our family and closest friends. Substitute sweet potato, parsnip, or carrot puree for the squash and we can assure you, the results will be just as successful.

SPONGE SHEET

1 acorn squash (about 1 pound)	1 teaspoon cinnamon
¼ cup all-purpose flour	½ teaspoon ground cloves or allspice
1 teaspoon baking powder	¼ teaspoon freshly grated nutmeg
5 large eggs, separated, at room temperature	⅛ teaspoon salt
¾ cup granulated sugar	⅛ teaspoon cream of tartar
1 teaspoon powdered ginger	Confectioners' sugar for dusting

FILLING

1½ cups heavy (whipping) cream	1 cup chopped crystallized ginger
2 tablespoons confectioners' sugar	

Preheat the oven to 350°F.

Cut the acorn squash in half and scrape and discard the fibers and seeds. Place the halves, cut side down, in a baking pan and bake in the center of the oven for 40 to 50 minutes, or until very tender and easily pierced by a fork. Scoop out all the pulp and puree in a food processor by pulsing several times, scraping down the sides and pulsing again. Set aside 1 cup to cool completely, saving the remainder, if any, for another use.

Meanwhile, butter a 16 × 11-inch jelly roll pan, line it with wax paper, and butter and lightly flour the wax paper.

On a large square of wax paper, sift together the flour and the baking powder. In the large bowl of an electric mixer set at high speed, beat the egg yolks for about 3 minutes, until light and frothy. Gradually beat in ½ cup sugar and continue to beat for

2 or 3 minutes more, or until the mixture ribbons when the beaters are lifted. On low speed, fold in the acorn squash puree, the flour mixture, ginger, cinnamon, cloves, and nutmeg. Beat until all ingredients are just combined. Set aside.

In another bowl of the mixer set at high speed, beat the egg whites with the salt and cream of tartar until they hold soft peaks. Gradually beat in the remaining ¼ cup sugar, a tablespoon at a time, and beat the whites until they hold stiff peaks.

With a rubber spatula, fold one-fourth of the whites into the squash mixture gently but thoroughly. Fold the remaining whites into the mixture gently until there are no traces of white left. Pour and scrape the batter into the prepared pan and spread it evenly with the spatula. Bake in the center of the oven for 20 minutes, or until the sponge sheet shrinks from the sides of the pan. Cool on a rack in the pan for 30 minutes, then invert onto a clean sheet of wax paper lightly sprinkled with confectioners' sugar. Lift off the pan and carefully peel away the wax paper from the inverted sponge sheet.

In the chilled bowl of an electric mixer on medium speed, beat the heavy cream until it thickens. Add the confectioners' sugar and continue to beat until the cream holds stiff peaks. With a spatula, fold in the crystallized ginger. Spread the cream mixture evenly over the sponge sheet, leaving a ½-inch border all around. Lifting the wax paper to help roll up the log, roll tightly lengthwise onto a fresh piece of wax paper placed parallel to the log. Using the wax paper as a sling, transfer the log, seam side down, to a rectangular serving platter or a long wooden paddle. Remove the wax paper and dust the log generously with confectioners' sugar. The log may be brought to the table immediately but it is even better if chilled for several hours before serving in 1½- to 2-inch slices.

Note ■ Don't worry if the cake cracks when you roll it up. The cracks can be disguised with the dusting of confectioners' sugar.

We don't like to lose a crumb of this cream log, but some cooks cut ½ inch of (what they think is unsightly, we think is delicious) crust from each end before presenting it. Of course it does look neater—but, then again, there's less to go around.

DELICATELY SPICED ZUCCHINI CREAM ROLL

Serves 8 to 10

$\mathcal{W}$e admit that unless we have something sweet after a meal, we're left hanging. But how to satisfy that craving and keep it light is often a problem. This gossamer cream roll is pleasantly sumptuous without being blatantly rich. Even after a heavy meal there always seems room for it. We vary the servings from 1 inch to 1½ inches thick, however, trying to be quietly sensitive to what has been served before. Guests can ask for more. And they invariably do.

ROLL

½ cup all-purpose flour

½ cup cornstarch

1 teaspoon baking powder

1 teaspoon powdered ginger

1 teaspoon cinnamon

½ teaspoon ground cloves

   Pinch of freshly grated nutmeg

5 large eggs, separated, at room
   temperature

¾ cup granulated sugar

1 cup grated zucchini (2 small, about
   ½ pound)

   Grated zest of 1 lemon

   Pinch of salt

⅛ teaspoon cream of tartar

   Confectioners' sugar for dusting

FILLING

1½ cups heavy (whipping) cream

2 tablespoons confectioners' sugar

1 tablespoon pure vanilla extract

Preheat the oven to 350°F.

Butter a 16 × 11-inch jelly roll pan and line it with wax paper. Butter the wax paper and dust it with flour, shaking out the excess. Set aside.

On a square of wax paper, sift together the flour, cornstarch, baking powder, ginger, cinnamon, cloves, and nutmeg. Set aside.

In the large bowl of an electric mixer, beat the egg yolks at high speed for about 3 minutes until they are frothy. Still at high speed, gradually add ½ cup granulated sugar and continue to beat the mixture about 3 minutes longer. Turn the mixer to low and fold in the grated zucchini, the lemon zest, and the flour mixture. Continue beating until all ingredients are thoroughly combined. Set aside.

In a separate bowl with the mixer at high speed, beat the egg whites, salt, and cream of tartar until they hold soft peaks when the beaters are lifted. Gradually beat in the remaining ¼ cup granulated sugar a tablespoon at a time until the whites hold stiff peaks.

With a rubber spatula, fold one-fourth of the whites into the zucchini mixture gently but thoroughly. Fold in the remaining whites until there are no traces of white in the mixture.

Pour the batter into the prepared jelly roll pan and spread evenly with a spatula. Bake in the center of the oven for 30 minutes. Invert onto a sheet of wax paper sprinkled with confectioners' sugar and carefully peel the wax paper from the inverted cake. Let cool for 20 minutes.

Meanwhile, in the chilled bowl of an electric mixer, beat the heavy cream at medium speed until it thickens. Add the confectioners' sugar and continue to beat until the cream holds stiff peaks. Beat in the vanilla.

Spread the filling evenly over the cake, leaving a ½-inch border on all sides. Starting with the long side, roll the cake tightly, lifting it with the wax paper to help you roll, finishing with the seam side down. Using the wax paper as a sling, transfer to a serving platter or board. Remove the wax paper carefully and trim the ends, if you like. Dust the roll with additional confectioners' sugar.

1-2-3-4 GINGER CHEESECAKE

Serves 12 to 14

*t*hose numbers in the title count up the four kinds of ginger used in this universally loved cheesecake. Count 'em: gingersnaps, fresh gingerroot, crystallized ginger, and ginger marmalade. It may sound like overkill to some, but not to those who taste it—even those who profess to dislike ginger. But if you're reticent and would rather scale back to just the two most important gingers (fresh and crystallized) and substitute chocolate wafers for the gingersnaps and a chocolate glaze (page 71) for the ginger marmalade, the result will receive the same amount of applause. Trust us on both versions.

CRUST

1 cup crushed gingersnaps

3 tablespoons unsalted butter, melted

FILLING

4 8-ounce packages cream cheese, at room temperature

½ cup heavy (whipping) cream

4 large eggs, at room temperature

1½ cups granulated sugar

1 teaspoon pure vanilla extract

2 tablespoons grated peeled fresh gingerroot

1 cup finely chopped crystallized ginger

TOPPING

2 tablespoons ginger marmalade (available at many supermarkets and specialty food stores) or more, to taste

Preheat the oven to 350°F.

Butter the inside of a metal cheesecake pan 8 inches across and 3 inches deep, or a round 8 × 3-inch cake pan (don't use a springform pan; it will leak in the water bath). In a medium bowl, combine the crushed gingersnaps and melted butter, mixing well with a fork. Press the crumb mixture into the bottom of the pan and halfway up the sides. Bake in the middle of the oven for 10 minutes. Set aside on a wire rack to cool.

Reduce the oven heat to 300°F.

In the large bowl of an electric mixer set at moderately high speed, beat the cream cheese, heavy cream, eggs, sugar, vanilla, and the grated gingerroot for 2 to 3 minutes, or until thoroughly combined and very smooth. With the mixer on low speed, blend in the chopped crystallized ginger.

Pour the batter into the prepared pan and gently shake or tap the pan on a work surface to level the mixture. Set the pan into a larger, low-sided pan such as a roasting pan. Be sure the edges of the pans do not touch. Place on the center rack of the oven. Pour boiling water into the larger pan to a depth of 2 inches. Bake for 1 hour and 40 minutes. Turn off the oven and let the cake rest in the oven 1 hour longer with the oven door slightly ajar.

Lift the cake pan out of the water and place it on a rack to cool at least 2 hours before unmolding. To unmold, run a sharp knife around the edges of the cake, invert a flat round cake plate over the pan, and carefully turn both upside down. Place a serving plate over the bottom of the cake and invert the cake, right side up, onto the serving plate. With a metal spatula, spread the top of the cake with the ginger marmalade. Keep the cake well chilled until 1 hour before serving.

ESPRESSO FENNEL CHEESECAKE

Serves 12 to 14

*t*hat inspired combination of flavors that Italians dote on, coffee and anise, crops up again, this time in a luscious cheesecake. The fennel adds just the right licorice flavor, just the right chewy surprise to the rich, elegant coffee filling. This recipe is a snap if you make the graham cracker crust ahead and chop and sauté the fennel while the crust is baking. Then whenever you're ready, whip together the cheese, espresso, sugar, and eggs and, except for the oven time, it's done.

CRUST

1 cup finely ground graham cracker crumbs

3 tablespoons unsalted butter, melted

FENNEL MIXTURE

1 tablespoon unsalted butter

1 fennel bulb (about ¾ pound), trimmed and cut into ¼-inch dice

1 tablespoon water

1 tablespoon Sambuca, Pernod, anisette, or other licorice-flavored liqueur

2 tablespoons granulated sugar

CHEESE FILLING

1 tablespoon espresso powder dissolved in 1 tablespoon hot water

4 8-ounce packages cream cheese, at room temperature

1½ cups granulated sugar

4 large eggs, at room temperature

1 tablespoon Sambuca, Pernod, anisette, or other licorice-flavored liqueur

Confectioners' sugar for dusting

Preheat the oven to 350°F.

In a medium bowl, combine the graham cracker crumbs with the melted butter, mixing well with a fork. Press the mixture evenly into the bottom of a metal cheesecake pan 8 inches across and 3 inches deep, or a round 8 × 3-inch cake pan (don't use a springform pan; it will leak in the water bath). Bake the crust in the center of the oven for 10 minutes. Set aside on a wire rack to cool.

In a medium saucepan set over moderately high heat, melt the butter and when the foam subsides add the fennel and sauté, stirring occasionally, for 5 minutes, or until the fennel is softened and coated with the butter. Add the water, the Sambuca, and the sugar and cook, stirring occasionally, for 5 minutes more, or until the liquid is completely absorbed. Set aside to cool.

Reduce the oven heat to 325°F. (Or, if the crust was made ahead, preheat the oven to 325°F.)

In the large bowl of an electric mixer set at moderately high speed, beat together the dissolved espresso powder, cream cheese, sugar, eggs, and Sambuca for 2 or 3 minutes, or until thoroughly combined and smooth. Reduce the speed to low and fold in the reserved fennel mixture. Pour the batter into the prepared pan and shake gently or tap the pan on a work surface to level the mixture. Set the pan into a larger, low-sided pan such as a roasting pan. Be sure the edges of the pans do not touch. Place on the center rack of the oven. Pour boiling water into the larger pan to a depth of 2 inches. Bake for 1½ to 2 hours, or until the top of the cake is pale golden in color. Turn off the heat and let the cake rest in the oven 20 minutes longer with the oven door slightly ajar.

Lift the cake pan out of the water and place it on a rack to cool *completely*, at least 2 hours or longer, if necessary, until set and firm. (The cake will unmold perfectly only if completely cooled. However, do *not* refrigerate in the pan in order to hurry the cooling or the cake will stick.) To unmold, run a sharp knife around the edge of the cake, place a flat round cake plate over the pan, and carefully turn both upside down. Place a serving plate over the bottom of the cake and invert the cake, right side up, onto the serving plate. Sprinkle the top with confectioners' sugar and serve.

UNBEETABLE MARBLEIZED ORANGE CHEESECAKE

Serves 12 to 14

*i*f you've ever made or eaten a marbleized raspberry cheesecake you know just what this cheesecake will look like. It's because that cake is so pretty in pink—and white—that we were inspired to try this one. But beets, being beets, retain their chewiness even when cooked and pureed. That texture, along with their distinctive sweetness and color, mingles with the smooth softness of the orange zest–flavored cream to create a stimulating new treasure for cheesecake lovers.

CRUST

1 cup chocolate wafer crumbs

3 tablespoons unsalted butter, melted

FILLING

4 8-ounce packages cream cheese, at
   room temperature

4 large eggs, at room temperature

1½ cups granulated sugar

Grated zest of 1 orange

½ cup Fresh Beet and Orange Jam
   (page 177), at room temperature

Preheat the oven to 350°F.

In a medium bowl, combine the chocolate wafer crumbs with the melted butter, mixing well with a fork. Press the mixture evenly into the bottom of a metal cheesecake pan 8 inches across and 3 inches deep, or a round 8 × 3-inch cake pan (don't use a springform pan; it will leak in the water bath). Bake the crust in the center of the oven for 10 minutes. Set aside on a wire rack to cool.

Reduce the oven heat to 325°F. (Or, if the crust was made ahead, preheat the oven to 325°F.)

In the large bowl of an electric mixer set at moderately high speed, beat together the cream cheese, eggs, sugar, and orange zest for 2 or 3 minutes, or until thoroughly combined and smooth. Set aside.

In a medium bowl, mix together the beet and orange jam with one-third of the cheese batter with a wooden spoon until the mixture is completely blended.

Place a large spoonful of the cheese batter on the cooled chocolate crust in the prepared pan and spread with a rubber spatula to cover. Place small spoonsful of the beet jam batter over this, with a few near the rim. Add more cheese batter and the remainder of the beet batter. Draw the rubber spatula through the two batters in a zigzag pattern or in a spiral to marbleize the two batters but not mix them. Set the pan into a larger, low-sided pan such as a roasting pan, making sure the edges of the pans do not touch. Place on the center rack of the oven. Pour boiling water into the larger pan to a depth of 2 inches. Bake for 1½ to 2 hours, or until the top of the cake feels set when pressed lightly with a finger. Turn off the heat and let the cake rest in the oven 20 minutes longer with the oven door slightly ajar.

Lift the cake pan out of the water bath and place it on a rack to cool completely for at least 2 hours or longer, if necessary, until set and firm before unmolding. (The cake will unmold perfectly only if completely cooled. However, do not refrigerate in the pan in order to hurry the cooling or the cake will stick.) To unmold, run a sharp knife around the edge of the cake, place a flat round cake plate over the pan, and carefully turn both upside down. Place a serving plate over the bottom of the cake and invert the cake, right side up, onto the serving plate. Serve chilled or at room temperature.

ITALIAN BEET GREEN CHEESECAKE

Serves 10 to 12

*t*his cheesecake recipe, in which the beet greens or Swiss chard provide a wonderful flavor, was passed on to us by Henny and Larry Nunno (good friends who love to eat), who first ate it at the home of their good friends Sergio and Rossella D'Argenio in the Tuscan coastal town of Sant' Andrea. We translated the recipe here as best we could and adapted it for the American kitchen. The result was as fragrant and glowing as Larry and Henny said it would be.

Beets are called *bietola* in Italian. But so is Swiss chard (a close relative), and beet leaves and Swiss chard are interchangeable in Italian cooking. Sergio and his wife actually made the original with Swiss chard. You can use either one. Thoroughly confused? One bite and you won't be.

CRUST

2½ cups blanched almonds (about 8 ounces), finely chopped

3 tablespoons granulated sugar

4 tablespoons (½ stick) unsalted butter, melted

FILLING

1 pound ricotta cheese, at room temperature

2 cups sour cream

3 large eggs, at room temperature

⅔ cup granulated sugar

1 tablespoon pure vanilla extract

10 large fresh beet leaves or Swiss chard without stems, rinsed, drained, patted dry with paper towels, and finely chopped (about 2 cups firmly packed)

Preheat the oven to 400°F.

Combine the chopped nuts and sugar in a 9- or 9½-inch springform pan, stir in the butter, and mix well. With your fingers or a wooden spoon, press the nut mixture firmly and evenly over the bottom and halfway up the sides of the pan. Bake for 5 to 8 minutes, or until golden brown. Place the pan on a wire rack to cool.

Reduce the oven heat to 350°F.

In the large bowl of an electric mixer at medium speed, beat the ricotta cheese, sour cream, eggs, sugar, and vanilla for about 2 minutes, or until thoroughly combined and smooth. Turn the speed to low and add the beet leaves, beating until just combined. Pour the batter into the prepared pan and bake for 1½ to 2 hours, or until firm. Place on a wire rack to cool. Chill in the refrigerator for at least 3 hours or overnight. Before serving, remove the sides of the pan and transfer the cake, on the bottom of the springform pan, to a cake platter or footed cake stand.

Note ■ This cake is quite rich, but if you like, it can be decorated with Amaretto-flavored whipped cream rosettes and sliced almonds.

TORTES

Experts define a torte as a cake made without flour. Usually, ground nuts or bread crumbs replace the flour. Not in our tortes. We use starchy vegetables instead. Our chestnut torte, for example, contains no chestnuts. We exchange expensive marrons glacés (glazed chestnuts) for our own economy version made with chickpeas. Cheaper, better tasting, more nutritious by far. And so we named it The Chestnut Torte That Isn't.

By the way, all the tortes in this chapter are more nutritious than they would be if made with nuts or bread crumbs. Vegetables are funny that way.

There is flour, however, in the Best Ever Linzer Torte. That's because the linzer torte is misnamed. Blame it on some long-forgotten Viennese who probably didn't have access to a dictionary. If he had looked it up he would have discovered that it really isn't a torte at all. It's more like a huge cookie or tart. But it has always been called a torte, so it ended up here.

Chocolate Velvet Torte ■ *Best Ever Linzer Torte* ■ *The Chestnut Torte That Isn't* ■ *Can't Be Beet Chocolate Nut Torte* ■ *Chocolate-Glazed Pois Chiches Glacés Torte with Liqueured Whipped Cream* ■ *Carrot Torte with Lemon Satin Glaze*

CHOCOLATE VELVET TORTE

Serves 6 to 8

*f*lo, Sally's mother, thinks this cake needs whipped cream to cut the richness. This may sound like an oxymoron, but it's so rich and fudgy that it does need a dollop of whipped cream or maybe a scoop of coffee ice cream, if only for contrast.

6 ounces best-quality bittersweet chocolate

2 tablespoons strong brewed coffee

½ cup (1 stick) unsalted butter

¾ cup plus 1 tablespoon granulated sugar

3 eggs, separated, at room temperature

⅓ cup ground pistachios, walnuts, or pecans

1 tablespoon pure vanilla extract

1 cup black bean puree, made from unseasoned home-cooked or canned beans (rinsed and drained)

Confectioners' sugar for dusting

Preheat the oven to 350°F.

Butter an 8-inch round cake pan.

In a small, heavy saucepan over the lowest possible heat, melt the chocolate with the coffee. Stir to combine and set aside to cool.

In the large bowl of an electric mixer set on medium speed, cream the butter and ¾ cup sugar together until light and lemon colored. Beat in the egg yolks one at a time, beating well after each addition. Add the cooled chocolate mixture, nuts, vanilla, and bean puree to the egg yolk mixture and beat at low speed until just combined.

In a separate bowl with an electric mixer or hand mixer, beat the egg whites until soft peaks form. Add the remaining tablespoon sugar and continue beating until stiff peaks form. With a rubber spatula, fold one-third of the egg whites gently but thoroughly into the batter to lighten it. Gently fold in the remaining whites until no flecks of white can be seen. Pour the batter into the cake pan, smoothing the top with the spatula, spreading it to the rim of the pan. Bake in the center of the oven for 1 hour. The middle of the torte may jiggle slightly when the pan is shaken, but it is meant to be quite moist.

Cool in the pan on a rack for 10 minutes. Run a small, sharp knife around the edge of the pan, cover with a serving plate, and invert the torte onto the plate. Dust the top with confectioners' sugar and serve in small wedges with or without a dollop of unsweetened whipped cream.

BEST EVER LINZER TORTE

Serves 8 to 10

*b*etter than Demel's in Vienna? That's what our friends say, even those who have eaten linzer torte in that hallowed spot, chosen from the endless array of opulent creations displayed on the long, tiered marble counter in that rococo temple of pastry making. We know we sound immodest to set ourselves above the kitchens of the official supplier of desserts to the former imperial Hapsburg family, but as the saying goes, "If you've got it, flaunt it!" Now you can flaunt it, too. And after your friends and family rave, tell them that what makes *your* linzer torte great is *beets*. Beets!? Yes, beets.

1½ cups unblanched (skins on)
     almonds
2 cups all-purpose flour
2 tablespoons cocoa powder
⅛ teaspoon ground cloves
¼ teaspoon cinnamon
1 cup (2 sticks) unsalted butter,
     softened

1 cup granulated sugar
1 teaspoon pure vanilla extract
3 egg yolks, at room temperature
1½ cups Fresh Beet and Orange Jam
     (page 177), at room temperature
1 egg white, at room temperature

In a blender, food processor, or nut grinder, finely grind the almonds until they are almost a powder. In a large bowl with a wooden spoon, mix together the ground almonds, flour, cocoa, cloves, and cinnamon until completely blended. Make a well in the center of the mixture and into it place the butter, sugar, and vanilla; gradually incorporate them into the almond mixture with the wooden spoon. When completely incorporated, add the egg yolks one at a time, beating well after each addition, until a soft dough is formed. Divide the dough in half and pat half the dough into a 9-inch fluted tart pan with a removable bottom, pushing the dough up the sides to form a ½-inch-thick wall around the edge. Flatten the remaining half of the dough into a circle between two sheets of wax paper. Refrigerate both the prepared tart pan and the dough circle for at least 1 hour or up to 24 hours.

Preheat the oven to 350°F.

Remove the tart pan from the refrigerator and with a metal spatula or spoon, fill the tart with the Beet and Orange Jam. Remove the chilled dough circle from the refrigerator and quickly roll it between the wax paper into a circle about 9 inches across. With a sharp knife or pastry wheel, cut it into ¼-inch strips. Arrange the strips in a lattice over the jam, pressing the edges lightly onto the wall of the tart with the tines of a fork. Beat the egg white with a fork until frothy and brush it over the lattice and border. (The torte can be refrigerated at this point for up to 24 hours, or until you are ready to bake it. Alternatively, it can be frozen for up to 2 weeks and partially thawed before baking.) Bake in the center of the oven for 50 minutes, or until it is lightly browned. Set on a rack to cool. Serve cut in wedges at room temperature.

THE CHESTNUT TORTE THAT ISN'T

Serves 8 to 12

*t*his torte is the great impersonator. Chestnuts are expensive, often difficult to find, and not a bit more flavorful than our economical, homemade impostors, chickpeas. This recipe makes a three-layer loaf cake, filled and smothered in pretend chestnut creme and decorated with chocolate shavings. It looks like it's for special occasions, but it's so easy to make and so economical that you can impress your family with it any day.

2   pinches of salt
1   teaspoon very cold water
10 egg whites

¾   cup granulated sugar
¼   cup all-purpose flour
½   cup finely ground walnuts

FAUX CHESTNUT FILLING
1   recipe Pois Chiches Glacés (page
      173), drained, syrup reserved for
      another use
¼   pound semisweet chocolate bits
½   pound (2 sticks) plus 2 tablespoons
      unsalted butter

¾   cup granulated sugar
1   teaspoon pure vanilla extract
1   large egg, at room temperature
¼   cup light rum

½   cup grated good-quality semisweet
      or bittersweet chocolate, shaved or
      grated, for decoration

Preheat the oven to 375°F.

Line a 17 × 12-inch baking sheet with wax paper. Butter the paper lightly and sprinkle with flour, shaking off the excess. Set aside.

In the bowl of an electric mixer set at medium speed, whip 1 pinch of salt, the water, and the egg whites until they form soft peaks. Turn the speed to moderately high and continue to beat, adding the sugar, a tablespoon at a time until the egg whites are so stiff that a spoon can stand straight up in them. Turn the mixer to low speed and gently fold in the flour, ground walnuts, and the remaining pinch of salt until just combined, taking care not to break down the meringue. With a rubber spatula, spread the batter evenly into the prepared baking sheet. Bake in the center of the preheated oven for 15 to 20 minutes, or until firm and golden brown on top.

Set the baking pan on a rack to cool, covering the top of the cake with a sheet of wax paper to prevent a crust from forming. While the cake cools, prepare the filling.

Puree the Pois Chiches in a food processor.

In a small, heavy saucepan over very low heat, melt the chocolate.

With an electric mixer set at moderate speed, beat together the butter, sugar, vanilla, egg, and rum until the mixture is light and foamy. Add the melted chocolate and the pureed chickpeas and beat until thoroughly blended. Keep at room temperature for spreading.

When the cake is cool, cut lengthwise into three pieces. Transfer one layer to a serving plate or wooden paddle and spread with ¼ inch of the filling. Set the second layer on top and spread with ¼ inch of filling. Set the third layer on top and spread the top and sides of the torte with the remaining filling. Sprinkle the top and press into the sides the shaved or grated chocolate and chill in the refrigerator for 2 hours or more before serving.

Note ■ This cake can take several shapes and heights depending on how you cut the layers. You can have a low, square cake by cutting the cake in two equal halves crosswise. You can make a four-layer, short, rectangular loaf by cutting the cake in four equal parts crosswise. Or you can have a shorter, wider three-layer torte by cutting the cake in thirds crosswise. The shape can often depend on how many people you want to serve or the size and shape of your serving platter.

CAN'T BE BEET CHOCOLATE NUT TORTE

Serves 8 to 10

*h*ow often do you have a dessert whose main ingredient offers a quick, nonfattening source of energy, contains a storehouse of vitamins and minerals plus all the amino acids, and acts as a mild diuretic to counteract water bloat? Beets add these nutritional bonuses to this torte *and* make it taste good, look good, keep it moist for days, and help intensify that deep chocolate richness besides.

1 16-ounce can whole or sliced beets	⅓ cup fine dry bread crumbs (unseasoned)
4 ounces semisweet chocolate	
5 large eggs, separated, at room temperature	2 teaspoons grated lemon zest
	Pinch of salt
¾ cup granulated sugar	Chocolate Glaze (recipe follows)
1½ cups finely ground unblanched almonds (skins on)	

Preheat the oven to 350°F.

Drain the beets and puree them in a food processor. Transfer the puree to a fine sieve and set aside to drain again. (You should be left with slightly more than 1¼ cups drained puree.)

Butter a 9-inch springform pan and line the bottom with a round of wax paper or parchment cut to fit. Butter the paper and dust lightly with flour. Set aside.

In a small saucepan set over very low heat, melt the chocolate, and when partially melted, stir with a rubber spatula until smooth. Remove from the heat and set aside to cool.

In the large bowl of an electric mixer set on high speed, beat together the egg yolks and ½ cup sugar for 2 to 3 minutes, or until creamy and pale yellow. Turn the speed to low and add the cooled chocolate, mixing just to combine. Still on low speed, add the ground nuts, bread crumbs, drained pureed beets, and lemon zest and mix until thoroughly blended. Set aside.

In another clean bowl of an electric mixer set on high speed, beat the egg whites with a pinch of salt until they hold soft peaks; do not overbeat. Still on high speed, gradually add the remaining ¼ cup sugar and beat until the whites hold a shape but are not stiff and dry.

With a rubber spatula, gently fold the whites into the chocolate mixture in several additions, mixing only to incorporate. Pour the batter into the prepared pan and bake in the center of the oven for 1 hour, or until the torte begins to shrink away from the sides of the pan. Place on a wire rack and cool completely in the pan. When cool, run a thin, sharp knife around the edge of the torte to release it. Remove the sides of the pan and invert the torte onto a rack. Remove the pan bottom and peel off the wax paper. Cover the torte with a cake plate and invert the torte again. Spread the top and sides of the torte with Chocolate Glaze. Serve at room temperature or slightly chilled.

CHOCOLATE GLAZE

2 ounces semisweet chocolate

2 tablespoons dark rum or strong
    coffee

6 tablespoons unsalted butter,
    softened

In a small saucepan over very low heat, melt the chocolate with the rum or coffee. Remove from the heat and beat in the butter with a wire whisk until thoroughly blended. Place the pan in a bowl of ice water and continue beating until the mixture is completely cooled and spreadable.

CHOCOLATE-GLAZED POIS CHICHES GLACÉS TORTE WITH LIQUEURED WHIPPED CREAM

Serves 8

*t*his is a promise of luxurious riches quietly fulfilled. Quietly, we say, because richness is balanced with nutrition. Pleasure, the main justification for dessert, is there, of course, but also shots of fiber, proteins, vitamins, and minerals delivered as only chick-peas can. So the guilt is ever so slightly tempered—at least that's what we keep telling ourselves.

TORTE

2 cups Pois Chiches Glacés (page 173), drained, syrup reserved

½ cup (1 stick) unsalted butter, softened

4 tablespoons dark rum

10 ounces best-quality bittersweet chocolate, chopped and melted

6 large eggs, separated, at room temperature

¼ teaspoon salt

½ cup granulated sugar

CHOCOLATE GLAZE AND DECORATION

½ cup heavy (whipping) cream

6 ounces best-quality bittersweet chocolate, finely chopped

1 tablespoon dark rum

16 whole Pois Chiches Glacés for garnish

WHIPPED CREAM ACCOMPANIMENT

1 cup very cold heavy (whipping) cream

¼ cup reserved syrup from Pois Chiches Glacés

1 tablespoon Frangelico (hazelnut liqueur), Amaretto, or dark rum

To make the torte, preheat the oven to 350°F.

Butter a 9-inch springform pan, line the bottom with buttered wax paper, and dust the pan with flour, knocking out the excess.

Puree the Pois Chiches, butter, and rum in a food processor, scraping down the sides, until the mixture is smooth. Add the melted chocolate and pulse several times until the mixture is well combined. With the motor running, add the yolks one at a time. Transfer the mixture to a large bowl.

In a bowl with an electric mixer, beat the whites with the salt until they hold soft peaks. Beat in the sugar a little at a time and continue beating until the meringue holds stiff peaks. Whisk about one-fourth of the meringue into the chocolate mixture to lighten it, then fold in the remaining meringue gently but thoroughly. Pour the batter into the prepared pan, smooth the top with a spatula, and bake the torte in the middle of the oven for 50 to 60 minutes, or until the top is cracked.

Transfer the torte in its pan to a rack to cool for 5 minutes, remove the side of the pan, and invert the torte onto another rack. Carefully remove the bottom of the pan, peel off the wax paper, and invert the torte onto the first rack and let it cool completely. It will settle as it cools.

To make the glaze and decoration, in a small heavy saucepan over moderate heat, bring the cream to a boil. Remove the cream from the heat and mix in the chocolate, stirring until the chocolate is melted and thoroughly blended into the cream. Stir in the rum. Invert the torte onto a rack set over wax paper and pour the warm glaze over it, smoothing the top and letting the excess glaze drip down the side, smoothing this with a spatula to coat evenly. Garnish the top of the torte with 8 pairs of Pois Chiches. Let the torte stand for 2 hours, or until the glaze is set. Transfer the torte carefully to a serving platter.

Just before serving the torte, pour the cream into the chilled bowl of an electric mixer and with chilled beaters, beat it until it holds soft peaks. Beat in the reserved syrup and the Frangelico until the mixture holds stiff peaks.

Serve individual wedges of the torte with small dollops of whipped cream, one on either side of the point.

CARROT TORTE WITH LEMON SATIN GLAZE

Serves 8 to 12

*t*his carrot cake is made with pureed cooked carrots instead of the usual grated raw carrots. The whole technique is different from the carrot cakes you are used to—there is no oil in the batter, in fact, no shortening at all (except to generously butter the pan). Along with a little flour, it contains white bread crumbs, confectioners' sugar (not granulated), and ground nuts. The resulting texture is lighter, less dense than other carrot cakes we make or you have tasted—and more carroty. You can also make this torte with pureed beets, rutabaga, salsify, parsnip, or artichoke hearts. Try it with the carrots first, then experiment.

2 tablespoons unsalted butter (for the pan)	1 teaspoon cinnamon
6 large eggs, separated, at room temperature	½ cup finely ground almonds or hazelnuts
1½ cups confectioners' sugar	½ teaspoon baking powder
1½ cups pureed cooked carrots (unseasoned)	½ cup fresh white bread crumbs (unseasoned)
½ lemon, both grated rind and juice	¼ cup all-purpose flour
	Lemon Satin Glaze (recipe follows)

Preheat the oven to 375°F.

Generously butter a 9 × 3-inch round cake pan and set aside.

In a large mixing bowl, whisk the egg yolks and sugar together with a wire whisk until the sugar is well combined. Add the pureed carrots and lemon rind and juice to the egg mixture and whisk until blended.

With an electric mixer set on moderately high speed, beat the egg whites until they hold stiff peaks. On low speed, gently fold in the cinnamon, ground almonds, baking powder, bread crumbs, and flour. With a rubber spatula, fold one-third of the egg white mixture into the carrot mixture thoroughly to lighten it, then fold in the remaining egg white mixture very gently until just combined. Pour the batter into the prepared pan and bake in the center of the oven for 20 to 25 minutes, or until a cake tester inserted in the center comes out clean. Cool in the pan on a wire rack for 5 minutes. Invert onto the rack and invert again onto a cake plate. Pour Lemon Satin Glaze over the top, letting it dribble down the sides.

LEMON SATIN GLAZE

¼ pound confectioners' sugar
   Juice of ½ lemon

1½ tablespoons warm water

Whisk sugar and lemon juice with the warm water. Continue whisking until the glaze becomes shiny and satin smooth. Use immediately.

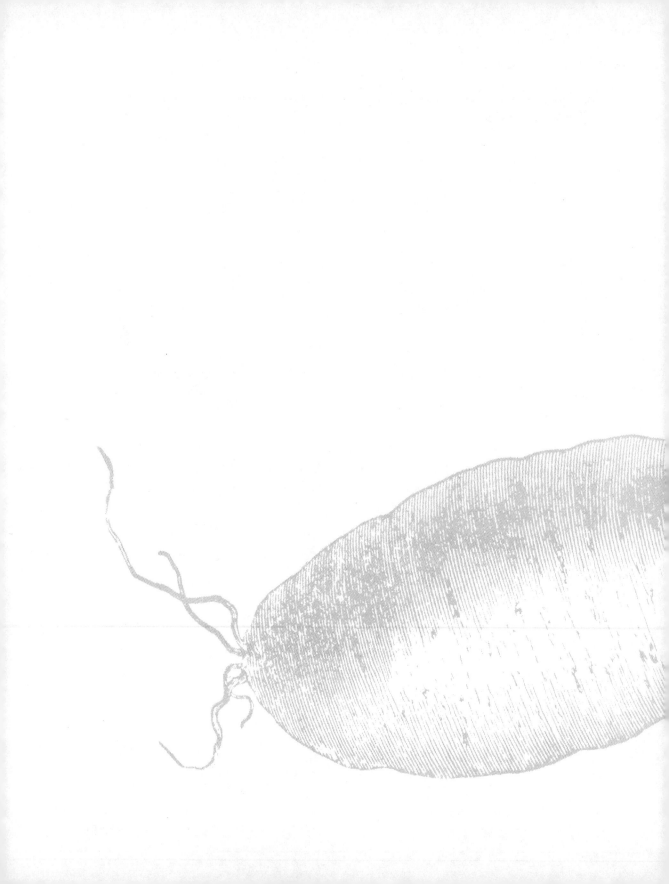

COOKIES

When it comes to cookies, some like them moist and chewy, others go for crisp or cakey. Here you will find something to please everyone. Black Beanies, brownies made with black bean puree instead of flour, are packed with nutritional necessities and are naturally moist and fudgy-textured because of the beans. Our chocolate chip cookies, with grated zucchini, will go over big with those partisans of chewy cookies. Vegetables usually keep baked goods moist—but only if the vegetables are pureed or grated fine. If they are chopped or diced, the batter surrounding them can become as crisp as you like.

A couple of tips: don't try to cool cookies on a flat surface. Moist or crisp, they'll turn limp and soggy from the steam they generate. Do use wire racks which allow air to circulate underneath. Always allow cookies to cool completely before storing in an airtight container. They'll stay fresh longer. Cookies freeze splendidly if wrapped well. Thaw them in their wrappings before serving.

Lace Cookies Laced with Ginger ■ *Ginger Chocolate-Chunk*

Five-Inch Cookies ■ *Zucchini Chocolate Chip Cookies* ■ *Golden*

Sweet Potato–Pecan Cookies ■ *Freckles* ■ *Black Beanies* ■

Crumbly Ginger Carrot Shortbread

LACE COOKIES LACED WITH GINGER

Makes about 6 dozen 2-inch cookies

*L*ace cookies always seem to stun guests. Normally intelligent people reveal their culinary ignorance with silly questions such as, "How do you get the holes in them?" or "There must be a special trick to these, right?" or "You bought these, didn't you?" The holes form during the baking process, making the cookies look fragile, exceedingly elegant, and, we must admit, difficult to make. This is far from the truth, however. The only "trick" is lifting them off the baking sheet at the exact moment they're ready. We tell you our method below. Even so, you may still lose a few at the beginning—but don't be discouraged, you'll quickly get the hang of it.

½ cup all-purpose flour	2 tablespoons heavy (whipping) cream
¼ teaspoon baking powder	2 tablespoons light corn syrup
½ cup granulated sugar	⅓ cup unsalted butter, melted
1 teaspoon powdered ginger	½ cup minced crystallized ginger
½ cup quick-cooking oats	1 tablespoon pure vanilla extract

Preheat the oven to 375°F.

In a medium bowl, sift together the flour, baking powder, sugar, and powdered ginger. Add the oats, heavy cream, corn syrup, melted butter, minced ginger, and vanilla and with a large spoon, mix together until well combined.

Using a ¼-teaspoon measuring spoon, scoop up the dough and drop it onto an ungreased baking sheet, placing the little mounds of dough about 4 inches apart.

Bake for 6 to 8 minutes, or until lightly browned. Remove the baking sheet from the oven and count to 10. Slide a metal spatula under each of the cookies to loosen them, and let them stand another few seconds until they begin to harden. With the spatula, transfer the cookies to a rack and let cool completely. Lace cookies will keep for a week if stored in an airtight container.

Note ■ You can spread these cookies when cool with a thin layer of melted semisweet chocolate, then press one of equal size and shape into the still soft chocolate to make a sandwich cookie—or dip about one-third of each cookie into melted semisweet chocolate and arrange on a rack over wax paper to catch the drips.

GINGER CHOCOLATE-CHUNK FIVE-INCH COOKIES

Makes about 30 5-inch cookies

*k*ids love things that are oversized or undersized. These cookies are definitely the former. Cookies for giants—or giant-sized appetites! Big enough for kids to share—if you can get them to. Of course, you could be a spoilsport and make them smaller (cut the baking time by a couple of minutes). The taste remains just as big.

1½ cups (3 sticks) unsalted butter, softened

1¼ cups firmly packed light brown sugar

1¼ cups granulated sugar

2 teaspoons pure vanilla extract

3 large eggs, at room temperature

3½ cups all-purpose flour

1½ teaspoons baking soda

1½ teaspoons salt

12 ounces good-quality semisweet or bittersweet chocolate, coarsely chopped (about 2 cups)

2 cups chopped crystallized ginger

Preheat the oven to 350°F.

In the large bowl of an electric mixer set on medium speed, cream the butter. With the mixer on, add the brown sugar and granulated sugar and beat the mixture until light and fluffy, about 3 minutes. Add the vanilla and continue beating until combined. Still beating, add the eggs one at a time, beating well after each addition.

Onto a sheet of wax paper, sift together the flour, baking soda, and salt. Add the dry ingredients to the butter mixture and beat on medium speed until well combined. On low speed, fold in the chocolate and crystallized ginger until completely distributed.

Drop level ¼ cupsful of the batter 3 inches apart on lightly greased cookie sheets. With wet hands, flatten the cookies into ½-inch-thick rounds. Bake in the center of the oven for 12 to 15 minutes, or until golden. Transfer the cookies to racks and let cool.

ZUCCHINI CHOCOLATE CHIP COOKIES

Makes 50 to 60 cookies

*J*oel Rapp, a friend and cookbook author, asked while we were testing this recipe, "Why make *zucchini* chocolate chip cookies? Are they that different from *regular* chocolate chip cookies?" Yes, of course they are. For one thing, they're much more nutritious (you can eat them—and all our vegetable sweets—with less guilt, more fiber, vitamins, and minerals); for another, they're moister, chewier, and keep longer, *and* they're one more way to use up that overachiever garden vegetable. But the best reason of all is that they are delicious.

½ cup (1 stick) unsalted butter, softened	1 teaspoon pure vanilla extract
1 cup firmly packed light brown sugar	1¼ cups all-purpose flour
1 large egg, at room temperature	1 teaspoon baking soda
1 cup grated zucchini	Pinch of salt
	1 cup chopped walnuts
	1 cup semisweet chocolate bits

Preheat the oven to 375°F.

In the large bowl of an electric mixer set on medium speed, cream together the butter and sugar until the mixture is light and fluffy. Beat in the egg until well blended. Add the zucchini and vanilla and continue beating until thoroughly incorporated. Reduce mixer speed to low and beat in the flour, baking soda, and salt until well combined. Add the walnuts and chocolate chips and mix to distribute well.

Drop the batter by rounded teaspoonsful, about 2 inches apart, onto ungreased cookie sheets. Bake in the middle of the oven for 8 to 10 minutes, or until the edges are golden brown and the cookies are firm to the touch. Transfer to a wire rack to cool (keep them separated or they might stick together). The cookies can be kept in an airtight container for several days.

GOLDEN SWEET POTATO-PECAN COOKIES

Makes about 36 cookies

You can make these cookies with drained canned "yams," but we like them best made with a large sweet potato baked on the oven floor (if, like ours, your oven's heat source comes from below) until it is charred. If you are in a hurry, though, steamed or canned will do almost as well. No matter what, the cookies come out a lovely golden color with a soft, moist texture. You might suspect that they'd be overly sweet, but they're not. They do have a southern kitchen, comforting quality about them that makes them perfect to serve on a cold afternoon in football season. We suggest glazing them, but they're almost as good without.

1¼ cups all-purpose flour

1½ teaspoons baking powder

1½ teaspoons baking soda

½ teaspoon salt

¼ teaspoon freshly grated nutmeg

¼ teaspoon ground coriander

4 tablespoons (½ stick) unsalted
   butter, softened

¾ cup firmly packed light brown
   sugar

1 large egg, at room temperature

1 cup pureed cooked sweet potato
   (about 1 large sweet potato,
   baked or steamed, or canned in
   syrup, drained and rinsed)

¼ teaspoon pure vanilla extract

Grated zest of 1 lemon

½ cup chopped pecans

LEMON GLAZE

1 cup confectioners' sugar

3 tablespoons lemon juice (juice of 1
   medium lemon)

36 pecan halves (optional)

Preheat the oven to 400°F.

On a large sheet of wax paper, sift together the flour, baking powder, baking soda, salt, nutmeg, and coriander. Set aside.

In the large bowl of an electric mixer set at moderately high speed, cream together the butter and brown sugar. When light and fluffy, beat in the egg, sweet potato puree, vanilla, and lemon zest. Reduce the speed to moderate and beat in the flour mixture until it is completely incorporated, about 2 minutes. Reduce the speed to low and fold in the pecans.

Drop by the tablespoonful 1½ inches apart onto buttered baking sheets and bake in the center of the oven for 12 to 15 minutes, or until golden brown. Lift from cookie sheets with a metal spatula and cool to just warm on wire racks while you make the glaze.

In a small bowl, whisk together the confectioners' sugar and lemon juice until it forms a spreadable paste. With a metal spatula, spread the glaze on the warm cookies. Lightly press a pecan half onto each cookie and cool completely.

FRECKLES

Makes 16 squares

*f*reckles could become as popular as brownies—moist, chewy, and dense. Here's finger food that seems too sumptuous not to be served on a plate and eaten with a fork. The combination of carrots, chocolate, brown sugar, and nuts is new. But you'll be saying, like most who taste them, "Where have these been all my life?"

½ cup (1 stick) unsalted butter, softened	1 cup all-purpose flour
	Pinch of salt, or to taste
1½ cups firmly packed dark brown sugar	¾ cup coarsely chopped pecans
	3 ounces semisweet chocolate bits
2 large eggs, at room temperature	1 cup grated carrots (about 3
1 tablespoon pure vanilla extract	medium carrots, peeled)

Preheat the oven to 350°F.

Butter a 9-inch square baking pan and set aside.

In the large bowl of an electric mixer set at medium speed, cream the butter and brown sugar until fluffy, about 2 to 3 minutes. Add the eggs one at a time, beating well after each addition. Beat in the vanilla. On low speed, add the flour and salt and beat only until mixed. Scrape down the sides of the bowl with a rubber spatula and, continuing on low speed, fold in the pecans, chocolate bits, and grated carrots. Mix until thoroughly combined.

Pour the batter into the prepared pan and bake in the center of the oven for 40 minutes, or until a cake tester inserted in the center comes out clean.

Allow to cool completely in the pan before cutting into 16 squares approximately 2¼ inches. You can also cut Freckles into smaller squares or into 2¼ × 3-inch bars.

BLACK BEANIES

Makes 36 1½ × 2-inch bars

*t*hese brownies are made with absolutely no flour. The grain is replaced by pureed black beans (we could have used other colors of kidney beans but black beans make these *appear* more richly chocolaty). Beans not only make Black Beanies more digestible to those who are allergic to grain but give the bars a moist, fudgy, velvety texture.

4 ounces (4 squares) unsweetened chocolate

1 cup (2 sticks) unsalted butter

4 large eggs, at room temperature

2 cups granulated sugar

1 cup black bean puree (see Note)

2 tablespoons instant espresso powder

1 cup chopped walnuts, pecans, or crystallized ginger

Preheat the oven to 350°F.

Butter a 9 × 13 × 2-inch baking pan.

In a small, heavy saucepan over the lowest heat possible, melt the chocolate with the butter. Stir to combine and set aside.

In the bowl of an electric mixer set on medium speed, beat the eggs one at a time into the sugar until light and lemon colored. Beat in the chocolate mixture until well combined. Beat in the bean puree along with the instant espresso powder and continue beating until the batter is smooth and the beans are completely incorporated. With a rubber spatula, fold in the walnuts and pour and scrape the batter into the pan. Smooth the top and bake in the center of the oven 55 to 60 minutes. Allow to cool completely before cutting into 1½ × 2-inch bars.

Note ■ We use bean purees made from dried beans, soaked 4 hours, drained, covered with 1 inch of water, and cooked without any seasoning or salt for 1½ hours, then drained and pureed in a food processor. Pureed or cooked beans can be kept frozen for a year.

However, canned beans are easier and just as successful for baking purposes. Before pureeing, drain the viscous liquid from the beans and rinse them in a sieve or colander under cold running water to remove as much of the salt as well as the oligosaccharides (undigestible sugars which cause flatulence or gas) as possible. Drain again and puree in a food processor. One 16-ounce can of beans will yield a scant 2 cups of puree.

CRUMBLY GINGER CARROT SHORTBREAD

Makes 16 1½ × 4-inch wedges

*W*e love shortbread. This one has a dry crumbly texture (we suggest it be eaten while leaning over a plate or else have the vacuum cleaner at the ready). It also has an intensely buttery taste, because we brown unsalted butter to a chestnut color in a small saucepan over moderately high heat, then pour it into a small heatproof container to resolidify in the refrigerator or freezer. This should be done at least 2 hours or up to 3 days ahead of time. Along with the zing of ginger and the sweetness of carrot, the browned butter imparts an appetizing golden color and offers an extra shot of flavor. Aside from this advance preparation, shortbread is easy to make: no electric mixer, no rolling pin—just a wooden spoon and your fingers. Satisfyingly back to basics.

¼ cup confectioners' sugar

¼ cup granulated sugar

1 cup (2 sticks) browned butter (see headnote for procedure), softened

⅓ cup rice flour (available in Asian groceries and health food stores)

1⅔ cups all-purpose flour

1 cup finely grated peeled carrots

1 tablespoon grated peeled fresh gingerroot

½ cup chopped crystallized ginger

Preheat the oven to 325°F.

In a large bowl mix the two sugars together with a fork. With a wooden spoon, cream the butter with the sugar mixture. Onto a large sheet of wax paper, sift together the two flours. With your fingertips or a wooden spoon, gradually incorporate the flour mixture into the sugar-butter mixture until the dough is smooth. Add the carrots and the two gingers and mix them into the dough until completely distributed.

Pat and press the dough evenly into a 9-inch metal tart pan with a removable bottom. With a sharp knife, score the dough deeply in half, then in half again. Divide the quarters in half, then in half again. You will have 16 wedges in all. Press all around the outer edge of the dough with the tines of a fork and bake in the middle of the oven for 1 hour, or until the shortbread is golden brown and somewhat springy to the touch. Let cool for 15 minutes on a wire rack, then remove the sides of the tart pan and let the shortbread cool completely on the rack.

PIES AND TARTS

A pie is an American variation on the European tart. Most of those you'll find recipes for here, by definition, must be first cousins once removed because instead of filling the crusts with fruits, berries, and nuts, we use vegetables. Consequently, few have any national historical background.

You'll find a couple of familiar friends in the group—pumpkin and sweet potato—both of which are vegetables, and both of which you surely are acquainted with. But for the most part our fillings will be new to you, at least in a pie: combined with other ingredients are mashed potatoes, tomatoes, beans, jicama, Swiss chard, parsnips, and carrots.

The pastry crust we use most often (page 112) is one Sally developed several years ago. It's a butter crust, but the butter is browned first and chilled back into solid form in the refrigerator or freezer before it is cut into the flour. The browned butter lends a nutty, even more buttery flavor to the crust than the classic, conventional crusts made with plain sweet butter or shortening.

We usually keep some browned butter in the freezer so that we can produce a pie dough on short notice. For the same reason, you might find rounds of well-wrapped dough there, waiting to be thawed and rolled out. Having a couple of partially baked crusts on hand as well (we usually do) lets you create a pie filled, baked, and out of the oven within an hour.

Tarts could be called open-faced pies, but the crust (page 114) is different—typically short, crisp, and delicate, cookielike. It can remain crisp for several days and won't get soggy from a moist filling. Again, to add flavor, we have substituted browned butter for the classic sweet butter in our crust. It does make a difference and is worth the tiny extra effort and planning.

One of our favorites made with this crust is the Basil Cream Fresh Raspberry Tart in which the pastry cream is flavored with fresh basil, an herb we find especially compatible with sugar and fruits.

We've also created a wonderful tart using the time-honored combination of rhubarb and strawberries—with our own addition of nuts for crunch and a sprinkling of cinnamon crumbs on top. If you were wondering why rhubarb is included here, it's because it is a vegetable, native to southeastern Russia and introduced to America right after the revolution, probably from Italy.

PIES ■ *Green Mountain Green Tomato Pie* ■ *Bourbon Street Sweet Potato Pie* ■ *Zucchini Custard Velours Pie* ■ *Zucchini-Walnut Brown Sugar Sweetie Pie* ■ *Pumpkin Sour Cream Chocolate Chip Pie* ■ *Sweet Potato and Orange Custard Pie in a Pecan Crust* ■ *Parsnip-Carrot Maple Pie with Crunchy Pecan Crust* ■ *Rustic Swiss Chard and Apple Pie* ■ *Rum Raisin Red Bean Cream Pie* ■ *Creamy, Crunchy Jicama Lime Pie* ■ *Jicama Sherry Pie with Broiled Cinnamon Topping*

TARTS ■ *Fennel Tart with a Hint of Almond and Lemon* ■ *Basil Cream Fresh Raspberry Tart* ■ *Red Cabbage Tart with Gingered Brown Sugar Pastry Cream* ■ *Elegant Carrot and Brown Sugar Tart* ■ *Rhubarb Strawberry Nut Tart with Cinnamon Crumb Topping* ■ *Brown Butter Piecrust* ■ *Brown Butter Sugar Crust*

GREEN MOUNTAIN GREEN TOMATO PIE

Serves 6

$f$rom the name you'd suspect that this pie was native to Vermont. Well, your suspicions would be correct. If you further suspected that Vermonters know their pies, taste this one and believe. The filling contains cider vinegar, which might turn you off at first glance. But be assured that the vinegar does not add a sour note; on the contrary, it works to sweeten this filling. Piquant is our word for it. We await your word.

Brown Butter Piecrust (recipe for a 2-crust pie, page 113)

6 green tomatoes (about 1½ pounds)

1 cup granulated sugar

½ teaspoon cinnamon

½ teaspoon allspice

¼ teaspoon ground cloves

¼ cup cider vinegar

2 tablespoons unsalted butter, cut into bits

Roll out one-half of the piecrust and press into a 9-inch pie pan. Chill the unbaked pie shell and the remaining dough (with any scraps) for 30 minutes.

Preheat the oven to 425°F.

When the pie shell has chilled, slice the tomatoes very thin. In a small bowl, combine the sugar, cinnamon, allspice, and ground cloves. Arrange half the tomato slices in the shell in one layer, sprinkle them with half the sugar mixture, pour half the vinegar over them, and dot them with half the butter. Repeat with the remaining tomatoes, sugar mixture, vinegar, and butter.

Roll the remaining dough into a round slightly larger than the pie tin. Moisten the edge of the shell and lay the round over the shell. Fold the overhang up over the round and flute the edges with your fingers to make a standing rim or press a crimped edge with a fork. With a sharp, pointed knife, cut a nickel-sized hole in the center of the top crust and cut several 1-inch-long slits around the vent like spokes. With any scraps of dough left over, you can cut leaves or circles and, first moistening the area around the vent, arrange them into a decorative edging surrounding it.

Bake the pie in the lower third of the oven for 20 minutes, reduce the heat to 375°F., and bake the pie for 40 minutes more. Transfer the pie to the upper third of the oven and bake it for 10 minutes more, or until the crust is nicely browned. Set the pie on a rack to cool until lukewarm and serve plain or with wedges of cheddar (preferably from Vermont) or with vanilla ice cream (try Ben & Jerry's, also from Vermont).

BOURBON STREET SWEET POTATO PIE

Makes one 9-inch pie

*I*f there is bourbon in a recipe it has to be southern. This pie is triply southern because it has bourbon, pecans, and sweet potatoes. One taste and you're transported to Creole New Orleans.

½ cup granulated sugar

1 teaspoon cinnamon

½ teaspoon allspice

½ teaspoon freshly grated nutmeg

½ teaspoon salt, or to taste

1 23-ounce can sweet potatoes, drained and mashed (about 1½ cups)

2 large eggs, lightly beaten

½ cup light cream or half-and-half

2 tablespoons unsalted butter, melted

¼ cup bourbon

Brown Butter Piecrust (recipe for a 1-crust shell, page 112)

24 or more pecan halves

Lightly sweetened whipped cream

Preheat the oven to 400°F.

In the bowl of an electric mixer set at medium speed, beat together the sugar, cinnamon, allspice, nutmeg, salt, sweet potatoes, and eggs until well combined. Beat in the cream, butter, and bourbon until well combined. Roll out the piecrust and press into a 9-inch pie pan. Pour the mixture into the unbaked pie shell. Arrange the pecan halves around the edge. Bake 40 minutes, or until a knife inserted into the center comes out clean. Serve warm or cooled to room temperature, topped with whipped cream.

Note ■ There's nothing wrong with serving this pie chilled if that's the way you like it. It just has a more intense flavor our way.

ZUCCHINI CUSTARD VELOURS PIE

Makes one 9-inch deep-dish pie serving 6 to 8

*t*his is an eggy-tasting, smooth-textured pie that can stand in for a pumpkin pie at Thanksgiving. It's quite light and subtle tasting, the perfect ending to a multicourse holiday meal. Of course, the Pilgrims did not serve zucchini at that first memorable harvest festival, but you can appease any sticklers for authenticity by recalling that both pumpkin and zucchini are from the squash family.

Brown Butter Piecrust (recipe for a 1-crust shell, page 112)

2 small zucchini, with skin, pureed raw in a blender or food processor (approximately 1 cup)

2 large eggs, separated

1⅓ cups milk

¼ cup granulated sugar

½ cup light brown sugar, lightly packed

1 tablespoon unsalted butter, melted

1 tablespoon light or dark rum

1 teaspoon cinnamon

Pinch of salt

3 tablespoons all-purpose flour

Preheat the oven to 425°F.

Roll out the piecrust into a 12- or 13-inch circle and lay it into a 9-inch *deep-dish* pie pan. Follow the directions for prebaking the pie shell.

In a medium bowl, combine the zucchini puree and egg yolks and whisk until well blended. Whisk in the milk, granulated and light brown sugars, butter, rum, cinnamon, and salt and combine well. Sift the flour over the mixture and whisk until smooth.

In another bowl, whisk the egg whites until they are shiny and form soft peaks. Whisk one-third of the whites into the zucchini mixture. Then, with a rubber spatula, gently but thoroughly fold in the remaining whites. Pour the filling into the prebaked pie shell.

Bake the pie in the center of the oven for 10 minutes, then reduce the heat to 350°F. and bake for 45 minutes longer, or until the custard is nearly set but still moves slightly in the center. Transfer to a rack to cool to room temperature before placing on a cake stand or pie platter and serving in generous wedges. It can also be served chilled.

Note ■ You may question the long baking time here. Because zucchini is watery the custard must bake longer than a similar pumpkin pie. If you substitute fresh or canned pumpkin puree for the zucchini, adjust the baking time downward to 25 to 30 minutes.

ZUCCHINI-WALNUT BROWN SUGAR SWEETIE PIE

Serves 8 to 10

*Y*ou've had pecan pies, you've had walnut pies, but you've never had a zucchini-walnut pie. Until now. Here, again, the vegetable works its magic to lighten and moisten and soothe an otherwise almost too cloyingly sweet dessert. No need to serve it with whipped cream to cut the sweetness, the zucchini does it for you. We bake it in a deep-dish, partially baked pie shell because the filling always seems to overflow a standard pie shell—even when we've cut back on quantities. We still bake this one on a cookie sheet just in case, because as delicious as this pie is, cleaning up burnt sugar syrup from the bottom of the oven is just not worth it.

Brown Butter Piecrust (recipe for a
   1-crust shell, page 112)
3 large eggs, at room temperature
¼ teaspoon salt
⅔ cup firmly packed brown sugar
1 cup light corn syrup

1 tablespoon light or dark rum
⅓ cup (5⅓ tablespoons) unsalted
   butter, melted
1 cup unpeeled grated zucchini
1 cup coarsely chopped or broken
   walnuts

Roll the piecrust into a 12- or 13-inch circle and lay it into a 9-inch *deep-dish* pie pan, then complete as instructed for prebaking the pie shell.

Preheat the oven to 375°F.

In the large bowl of an electric mixer set at moderately high speed, beat together the eggs, salt, sugar, corn syrup, rum, and melted butter. Turn the speed to low and beat in the zucchini and walnuts until just combined. Pour the filling into the prepared pie shell, place on a cookie sheet, and bake in the middle of the oven for 50 to 55 minutes, or until the filling is set and the top turns a golden brown. Transfer to a wire rack to cool; the center will sink slightly. Serve warm, at room temperature, or chilled.

PUMPKIN SOUR CREAM CHOCOLATE CHIP PIE

Serves 6

*W*e've had pumpkin pies made by some of the great bakers but none has ever tasted so good as the first pumpkin pie ever to pass our lips, from the now defunct Horn & Hardart Automats. The crust was awful—gummy and usually left on the plate. But what a filling! Too much cinnamon, too much pumpkin pie spice, too much of everything—in other words, perfect. This recipe brings back that same feeling we had when we first tasted that sublime, and to us, exotic, dessert. It's a shame that pumpkin pies are usually served only at Thanksgiving dinners. As far as we are concerned they can end any meal, any time, any season.

Brown Butter Piecrust (recipe for a
  1-crust shell, page 112)
2 large eggs, at room temperature
1 cup firmly packed light brown
  sugar
¼ teaspoon salt
1 teaspoon powdered ginger
2 teaspoons cinnamon

1 teaspoon pumpkin pie spice
¼ teaspoon freshly grated nutmeg
½ teaspoon ground cloves or allspice
2 cups home-cooked or canned
  pumpkin puree
1½ cups sour cream
¾ cup semisweet chocolate bits

Preheat the oven to 450°F.

Roll out the piecrust into a 12- or 13-inch circle and lay it into a 9-inch deep-dish pie pan. Follow the instructions for a fluted edge (page 113), then press all around the edge with your fingers a second time to make a *standing* fluted rim. Set aside.

In the large bowl of an electric mixer set on moderately high speed (or by hand with a wire whisk), beat the eggs with the sugar, salt, and spices until well blended. Add the pumpkin puree and sour cream and continue beating until thoroughly combined. With a rubber spatula, fold in the chocolate chips. Pour and scrape the mixture into the prepared pie shell, place on a cookie sheet, and bake on the lower rack of the oven for 10 minutes. Reduce the oven temperature to 400°F. and continue to bake 30 minutes more, or until a tester inserted into the center of the pie comes out clean. Cool to room temperature on a wire rack before chilling for 1 hour or more. This pie tastes equally good at room temperature or straight from the refrigerator. Serve it the way you and your family prefer.

SWEET POTATO AND ORANGE CUSTARD PIE IN A PECAN CRUST

Makes one 9-inch deep-dish pie serving 6 to 8

S weet potatoes and pecans are both southern. Using raw, grated sweet potatoes in a pie is unusual, but a satiny texture results. The pecans are not in the filling, but in the crust, offering a crunchy contrast. Because the crust is prebaked and the filling must be baked for 45 minutes to 1 hour, we suggest you have an aluminum foil collar handy to place over the pastry rim of the pie to prevent it from overbrowning. Pour any extra filling into a custard cup and bake along with the pie.

¾ cup (1½ sticks) unsalted butter

1 cup firmly packed dark brown sugar

2 large eggs, lightly beaten

2 cups peeled, grated raw sweet
   potato (about ¾ to 1 pound)

3 tablespoons grated orange zest

2 tablespoons orange liqueur
   (Cointreau, Triple Sec, or the like)

1 tablespoon lemon juice

½ teaspoon powdered ginger

½ teaspoon mace

¼ teaspoon freshly grated nutmeg

¼ teaspoon ground cloves

1 prebaked Crunchy Pecan Crust
   (page 97)

Preheat the oven to 350°F.

In the large bowl of an electric mixer set at medium speed, cream together the butter and brown sugar. Add the beaten eggs and grated sweet potato and continue to beat until well combined. Beat in the orange zest, orange liqueur, lemon juice, ginger, mace, nutmeg, and cloves until thoroughly incorporated. Pour half the custard mixture into the cooled prebaked pie shell, place the pie on a cookie sheet, and place in the bottom third of the oven. Pour in the remaining filling carefully until it barely reaches the rim of the crust. (Bake any excess custard in a custard cup along with the pie.) Bake for 45 to 50 minutes, or until the custard is firm when you shake the pan.

Let the pie cool to room temperature on a wire rack, then refrigerate for 1 hour or up to 24 hours before serving.

Note ■ If you make this pie the day before, remove it from the refrigerator and let it stand for 20 minutes or more before serving.

PARSNIP-CARROT MAPLE PIE WITH CRUNCHY PECAN CRUST

Makes one 9-inch deep-dish pie serving 6 to 8

*b*oth parsnips and carrots are sweet roots. Carrots have been used for sweet puddings and cakes for centuries. Parsnips were eclipsed by the introduction of the potato to Europe from the Andes in the sixteenth and seventeenth centuries and lost favor as a vegetable. Until then they were often served as a sweet to end a meal or to quiet a teething baby. We love them in cakes and pies. They have an underlying spicy flavor that marries well with other flavorings. The two roots combined with maple syrup, spices, and a nut-flavored and textured crust are an unexpectedly enjoyable way to get at least part of your daily ration of vegetables.

1 pound parsnips, peeled and cut in ½-inch dice

1 pound carrots, peeled and cut in ¼-inch rounds

1 cup half-and-half

3 large eggs, lightly beaten

¾ cup pure maple syrup

1 teaspoon maple extract

1 teaspoon cinnamon

1 teaspoon powdered ginger

¼ teaspoon ground cloves

⅛ teaspoon mace

½ teaspoon salt

1 prebaked Crunchy Pecan Crust (recipe follows)

Preheat the oven to 350°F.

On a steamer rack set over briskly boiling water, steam the parsnips and carrots for 12 to 15 minutes, or until they are very tender. Remove the steamer rack and let the vegetables cool and dry. Force them through a ricer or a food mill into a bowl or, alternately, puree them in a food processor. You should have about 2½ cups. Whisk the half-and-half into the puree until well blended. Whisk in the eggs, maple syrup, maple extract, cinnamon, ginger, cloves, mace, and salt until the filling is smooth.

Pour the filling into the prepared Crunchy Pecan Crust, smoothing the top with a rubber spatula. Bake the pie in the middle of the oven for 40 to 45 minutes, or until it is just set in the middle (to prevent overbrowning the rim of the crust you may want to cover the edge with an aluminum foil collar halfway through the baking time). Let cool on a wire rack. Serve at room temperature or slightly chilled and topped with vanilla ice cream or frozen yogurt or whipped cream. Pass more maple syrup at the table to drizzle over the pie and topping.

Note ■ You can make this pie with all parsnip or all carrot puree. Or substitute 2½ cups of cooked and pureed sweet potatoes or Jerusalem artichokes—or homemade or canned pumpkin puree. The other ingredients, the method, and serving suggestions remain the same.

CRUNCHY PECAN CRUST

This is a wonderful crust to use to hold dozens of refrigerated fillings—mousses, chiffons, custards. It will add nuttiness and texture to pumpkin, apple, pear, or peach pies. It can also be used for berry and fruit tarts. We sometimes add chocolate chips along with the nuts (walnuts, cashews, and Brazil nuts work equally well) depending upon the choice of filling.

1 cup pecans	½ teaspoon salt
2 tablespoons granulated sugar	3 tablespoons ice water
1½ cups all-purpose flour	
6 tablespoons (¾ stick) cold unsalted butter, cut into small pieces	

Preheat the oven to 425°F.

In a food processor, pulse the pecans with the sugar just until coarsely ground and transfer to a bowl. Without wiping out the food processor workbowl, process the flour, butter, and salt until the mixture resembles coarse meal. Add the flour mixture to the pecan mixture along with the ice water. With a fork, toss the mixtures together until the water is incorporated. Press the dough into the bottom and up the sides of a 9-inch deep-dish pie pan, crimping the edge decoratively with your fingers. Prick the crust all over with a fork and chill it for 30 minutes.

Line the crust with foil, fill with dried beans or raw rice, and bake the crust in the middle of the oven for 7 minutes. Remove the beans or rice and foil, and bake the crust for 5 minutes more. Let cool before filling.

RUSTIC SWISS CHARD AND APPLE PIE

Serves 6 to 8

S wiss chard is a favorite vegetable in Europe, especially in Provence. This pie with its
thick, farm kitchen–style bottom crust is one way French country cooks use it—and
have for years—unselfconsciously, for dessert. The pie is lovely and robust as is, but is
really impressive, yet still unpretentious, when accompanied by crème fraîche (recipe for
a homemade version follows) or with lightly whipped cream, sweetened and flavored with
Calvados or applejack.

FARM KITCHEN CRUST

1½ cups all-purpose flour

2 teaspoons baking powder

¼ teaspoon salt, or to taste

2 tablespoons granulated sugar

5 tablespoons light olive oil

8 tablespoons ice water

FILLING

⅓ cup golden raisins

3 tablespoons Calvados, applejack, or
brandy

1 pound Swiss chard leaves, tough
stems and center vein removed

1 large Granny Smith or Greening
apple

1 tablespoon pine nuts (pignoli),
chopped almonds, or chopped
unroasted cashews

2 vanilla wafers, crushed
Grated zest of ½ lemon

1 large egg, lightly beaten

2 tablespoons strawberry jam or
currant jelly
Confectioners' sugar for dusting the
pie
Homemade Crème Fraîche (recipe
follows)

Oil the inside of an 8-inch fluted tart pan with a removable rim.

Into a large bowl, sift together the flour, baking powder, salt, and sugar. Add the oil
all at once and with the tips of your thumbs and first two fingers of each hand, using a
sliding motion as if dealing cards or counting money, lightly and very quickly rub (do
not squeeze or press) the oil and the flour mixture together until it is just combined.
Immediately pour the ice water into the flour mixture and toss with a fork just until it
can be gathered into a moderately firm ball (if it still seems crumbly, sprinkle in an
additional *teaspoonful* of ice water, no more). Dust the ball of dough with flour, flatten
it, wrap in plastic wrap, and refrigerate for at least 30 minutes.

While the dough is chilling, soak the raisins in 2 tablespoons Calvados. Wash the Swiss chard leaves well, and in a sauté pan over moderate heat cook them in the water clinging to them, stirring occasionally, for 3 to 5 minutes, or until limp and tender. Drain any remaining liquid, chop coarsely, and separate the chopped leaves with a fork.

Peel and core the apple and slice it very thinly. Toss the apple with the Swiss chard, raisins and their Calvados, pine nuts, vanilla wafer crumbs, lemon zest, and beaten egg until well combined.

Preheat the oven to 350°F.

Cut off two-thirds of the chilled dough and, with a floured rolling pin, roll it into a circle at least 9 inches across, enough to line the tart pan. Transfer the dough by rolling it over the rolling pin and then laying it loosely into the pan. Gently lift small sections of the overhanging dough and, using a fingertip, carefully press the dough into the fluted sides of the tart pan without stretching it.

Fill the pastry shell with the Swiss chard mixture, mounding it slightly in the center. Thin the strawberry jam with the remaining tablespoonful of Calvados and spread the thinned jam over the surface.

Roll out the remaining dough into a circle large enough to slightly overlap the top; fold in half and then in half again. Dampen the edge of the pastry shell with water, lay the point of the quarter circle of dough in the center of the chard filling, and unfold. Roll the rolling pin over the edge of the tart pan both to cut the dough neatly and to form a tight seal. Let the excess dough fall off, press this into a ball, and roll out ⅛ inch thick. Cut into nickel-sized circles or small leaves. Cut a small hole in the center of the pie, dampen the edge with water, and surround the hole with overlapping small circles or leaves of dough. Make a small funnel from wax paper or foil and insert into the hole.

Place the tart pan on a baking sheet and bake in the center of the oven for 30 to 40 minutes, or until golden brown. Transfer to a rack, remove the funnel, and sprinkle the top with confectioners' sugar. Let cool on the rack until it can be handled and carefully remove the fluted ring from the pie by setting the tart pan on a small bowl deeper than the pan is high and gently pushing down on the ring to release it (you may need to use a small, sharp pointed knife to free reluctant pastry from the sides).

Transfer the pie on its metal disc to a serving platter. Serve warm or at room temperature with crème fraîche or Calvados-flavored whipped cream.

Note ■ This pie can be made with any two-crust pie recipe, although the result is not as rustic (read, *peasant*).

HOMEMADE CRÈME FRAÎCHE

Makes approximately 1 cup

Sour cream does not have the same taste as crème fraîche but in a pinch you can come close by thinning a commercial sour cream with a little milk. But if you have the time, this recipe is easy and the result is delicious, very French, and can be stored in the refrigerator for 4 to 6 weeks.

1 cup heavy (whipping) cream

1 or 2 tablespoons buttermilk

In a small jar, combine the cream and buttermilk, cover tightly, and shake well. Let the mixture sit near a pilot light (not on it) or in another warm place for 6 to 8 hours. Store in the refrigerator. Serve chilled.

RUM RAISIN RED BEAN CREAM PIE

Serves 6 to 8

One of the first great ice cream flavors to sweep the soda fountains of the Northeast in the 1930s was rum raisin. It was a truly exotic combination of flavors—and for kids, a way to taste the forbidden fruits of adulthood without going behind the woodshed to do it. Who knew then that the rum flavoring was imitation. Who cared? This unusual cream pie recreates, for us at least, that wonderful feeling of "a treat," a feeling, as jaded adults, we tend to forget. If you have forgotten, here's how to remember . . .

1 3-ounce package cream cheese

1 cup confectioners' sugar, sifted

¼ cup milk

1 cup kidney bean puree, made from unseasoned home-cooked or canned kidney beans (rinsed and drained), sieved to remove bits of skin

½ cup raisins plumped in 2 tablespoons dark rum

1½ cups well-chilled heavy (whipping) cream

3 tablespoons chopped rum cashews (see Note) or chopped pecans Graham Cracker Crumb Crust (recipe follows)

In the bowl of an electric mixer set on medium speed, beat the cream cheese with the confectioners' sugar until light and fluffy. Still beating, add the milk, the bean puree, and the raisins with their liquid.

In a chilled bowl with a hand-held beater or with an electric mixer, beat the heavy cream until it holds stiff peaks. Stir one-third of the whipped cream into the bean mixture until thoroughly combined, then with a rubber spatula fold in the remaining whipped cream gently but thoroughly. Mound the filling in the cooled crust and sprinkle with the rum cashews. Chill, covered lightly, for at least 4 hours or overnight.

Note ■ Rum cashews can usually be found at those specialty stores that scoop candy and nuts from big glass jars. They're simply cashews roasted with a sweet rum coating.

GRAHAM CRACKER CRUMB CRUST

Any cream, chiffon, or pudding filling is perfect to mound into a crumb crust like this. The contrast in texture between the crunchy crust and the ethereal filling is what you're after. Chopped nuts, chocolate chips, or crushed hard candies can be added to the crumb mixture, if you like, to complement both texture and taste.

1⅔ cups (about 12 crackers) graham cracker crumbs

¼ cup granulated sugar

6 tablespoons (¾ stick) unsalted butter, melted and cooled

Preheat the oven to 425°F.

In a medium bowl, stir together the crumbs, sugar, and melted butter until well combined. Press the mixture into a 9-inch pie pan and bake in the lower third of the oven until the shell darkens slightly. Cool on a wire rack before filling. (The crust may be made a day ahead and stored at room temperature—or it can be wrapped, airtight, and frozen for up to 3 months. Let thaw for at least ½ hour before filling.)

CREAMY, CRUNCHY JICAMA LIME PIE

Serves 6 to 8

Slices of raw jicama sprinkled with lime juice and dusted with a little chile powder is a refreshing companion to drinks. We wondered what the same combination, altered slightly, would be like in a dessert pie. The result told us to trust our instincts; when a combination of flavors works in one area, with only a little romancing, it can often (key word) work in another. This pie is made with a chocolate crumb crust, but there is no reason it couldn't be made with a vanilla wafer or graham cracker crust or a prebaked pie shell. We've topped ours with sweetened whipped cream, but you could use a lime-flavored meringue, if you'd rather not increase your cholesterol intake. It's even great topless.

4 large egg yolks, at room temperature

½ cup plus 1 tablespoon freshly squeezed lime juice (preferably Key limes) or bottled Key lime juice

1 teaspoon grated lime rind

1 14-ounce can sweetened condensed milk

½ teaspoon chile powder

½ pound jicama, peeled and coarsely shredded (about 2 cups)

1 Chocolate Crumb Crust for a deep-dish 9-inch pie pan (recipe follows)

1 cup well-chilled heavy (whipping) cream

3 tablespoons confectioners' sugar

Preheat the oven to 350°F.

In the bowl of an electric mixer set on medium speed, beat the yolks until they are light and lemon colored. Add ½ cup lime juice, grated rind, and condensed milk and beat until well combined.

Sprinkle the remaining lime juice and chile powder over the grated jicama, toss, then fold the mixture into the custard. Pour into the prepared pie shell and bake in the middle of the oven for about 25 minutes, or until the custard is almost set. Transfer to a rack and let cool completely. Chill for at least 1 hour or up to 24 hours before topping with the whipped cream.

In the well-chilled bowl of the electric mixer set on medium speed, beat the heavy cream until it holds soft peaks. Sift or sprinkle the confectioners' sugar over it and continue to beat until the cream holds stiff peaks. Spread the whipped cream with a spatula over the cooled pie filling, lifting the spatula to form decorative peaks. Serve the pie well chilled.

CHOCOLATE CRUMB CRUST

½ pound chocolate wafers, broken into
   pieces

4 tablespoons (½ stick) unsweetened
   butter, softened

Preheat the oven to 350°F.

Butter a 9-inch deep-dish pie pan.

In a food processor, pulse the chocolate wafer pieces and butter until finely crumbled and well combined. Press the mixture into the bottom and up the sides of the pie pan. Bake the crust on a baking sheet in the middle of the oven for 20 to 25 minutes. Remove and let cool on a rack before filling.

The crust may be made ahead and kept in an airtight container in the refrigerator for up to a week or in the freezer, tightly wrapped, for up to 2 months.

Note ■ You can gild this lily of a crust with chocolate. Just add ⅓ cup finely chopped semisweet chocolate to the crumbled wafer-butter mixture and proceed as above. Or, alternately, substitute ⅓ cup ground pecans, walnuts, hazelnuts, or lightly toasted ground blanched almonds.

For a children's party we once decorated the whipped cream topping with a sprinkling of crushed lime-flavored sour balls.

JICAMA SHERRY PIE WITH
BROILED CINNAMON TOPPING

Serves 6 to 8

i f this pie had been invented in this country it would most likely be made with apples. But in Mexico, where jicama is native and sherry is part of the Spanish heritage, their inclusion is natural. Try this *pastel* and discover the perfect ending to a Mexican meal.

½ pound jicama, peeled and coarsely shredded (about 2 cups)

½ cup sherry (dry or sweet)

½ cup water

¾ cup granulated sugar

6 tablespoons all-purpose flour

¼ teaspoon salt, or to taste

3 large egg yolks, at room temperature

2 cups milk

1 cinnamon stick

2 teaspoons unsalted butter

1 fully prebaked 9-inch Brown Butter Piecrust (recipe for a 1-crust shell, page 112)

CINNAMON TOPPING

½ teaspoon cinnamon

1 tablespoon sugar

1 tablespoon unsalted butter, cut into tiny pieces

In a small saucepan, combine the jicama, sherry, and water and bring to a boil. Reduce the heat to moderate and boil gently, covered, for 25 minutes, or until most of the liquid has evaporated, checking to make sure it doesn't scorch. Drain in a sieve, pressing out as much liquid as possible, and set aside.

In a medium saucepan, mix together the sugar, flour, and salt. In a small bowl, beat the egg yolks with 1 cup milk and whisk into the sugar mixture, whisking until smooth. Set the saucepan over moderate heat, add the remaining milk and cinnamon stick, and stir often until the mixture boils and becomes very thick. Remove from the heat, fold in the drained jicama, and cook 1 to 2 minutes longer. Remove from the heat and discard the cinnamon stick. Stir in the butter and let the mixture cool slightly before pouring into the prebaked pie shell. Smooth the top of the pie with a spatula.

Preheat the broiler. Combine the ground cinnamon and sugar and sprinkle evenly over the filling. Dot with the butter and broil 3 inches from the heat until the butter and cinnamon sugar melt and become bubbly. (You may need to cover the crust with a foil collar to prevent it from burning.) Cool the pie to lukewarm or to room temperature and serve.

FENNEL TART WITH A HINT OF ALMOND AND LEMON

Serves 10 to 12

*h*ere's another recipe in which none of the flavors are so intense that they eclipse any of the others. The tart is based on the memory of a classic French lemon-almond tart we loved long ago in Paris—with our own addition of fennel, licorice-flavored liqueur, and our best Brown Butter Sugar Crust. Recollections are faulty at best, but not when it comes to this tart. Memorable is the word!

1 small fennel bulb (about ½ pound), trimmed and cut into ¼-inch dice

4 large eggs, at room temperature

1 cup granulated sugar
   Grated zest of 2 lemons

1 cup blanched almonds, ground very fine

¾ cup (1½ sticks) unsalted butter, melted and cooled

2 tablespoons Sambuca, Pernod, anisette, or other licorice-flavored liqueur

1 unbaked Brown Butter Sugar Crust (page 114), fitted into a 10-inch tart pan with a removable bottom
   Confectioners' sugar for dusting

Preheat the oven to 400°F.

Combine the fennel with water to cover in a medium saucepan, and bring to a boil over moderately high heat. Lower the heat to a simmer and cook for 5 minutes, or until fennel is softened. In a food processor, puree the fennel with any liquid remaining in the pan and set aside to cool.

In the large bowl of an electric mixer set on high speed, beat together the eggs, sugar, lemon zest, and ground almonds until well blended. Turn the speed down to low and fold in the melted butter, pureed fennel, and Sambuca until completely combined.

Place the prepared tart pan on a cookie sheet, place on the middle rack of the oven, and pour in the filling. It will probably come to the very rim of the tart shell; do not overfill. Bake for 50 minutes, or until the filling is firm to the touch. Transfer to a wire rack to cool. Serve at room temperature sprinkled with confectioners' sugar or with a dollop of sweetened whipped cream on each wedge.

Note ■ This tart can be made several days in advance, covered lightly, and refrigerated.

BASIL CREAM FRESH RASPBERRY TART

Serves 6

*t*he two of us often disagree about how the results of a particular inspiration should taste. In this tart we anguished over whether the basil or the raspberries should predominate. When we finally baked it we realized that neither of the ingredients stood out, but instead they both melded to form a new flavor. It seems that we hit upon the perfect proportions of each so that neither is in control, neither is subservient—sort of like the perfect marriage.

PASTRY CREAM

1 cup (½ pint) half-and-half

½ cup firmly packed finely chopped
    fresh basil leaves

2 tablespoons all-purpose flour

⅛ teaspoon salt

½ cup granulated sugar

4 large egg yolks, at room temperature

1 teaspoon pure vanilla extract

GLAZE

½ cup currant jelly

2 tablespoons granulated sugar

1 tablespoon crème de cassis, kirsch,
    or cognac

1 fully prebaked Brown Butter Sugar
    Crust (page 114) for an 8-inch tart
    pan with a removable bottom

½ pint fresh unblemished raspberries

In a small saucepan set over moderately high heat, scald the half-and-half. Remove the pan from the heat and stir in the basil. Let the mixture stand for at least 5 minutes to develop flavor. Pour the mixture through a fine metal sieve into a small bowl or measuring cup, pressing hard on the basil to extract as much of its essence as possible. In a medium saucepan, whisk together the flour and ¼ cup basil cream until smooth. Gradually whisk in the remaining basil cream until completely combined. Whisk in the salt and sugar, set the pan over moderate heat, and cook, whisking, until the mixture is thickened. Remove from the heat. In a small bowl, whisk a little of the hot basil cream into the egg yolks, then pour this egg mixture back into the saucepan set over low heat and cook, whisking briskly, for 2 or 3 minutes longer, or until the mixture thickens even more. Be careful not to let the mixture boil. Remove the pan from the heat and whisk in the vanilla. Let the basil pastry cream cool completely before assembling. (This may be done up to a day ahead; keep refrigerated, and stir well before assembling the tart.)

To make the glaze, in a small saucepan set over moderately high heat, mix together the currant jelly and sugar and, stirring, bring to a boil. Remove the saucepan from the heat and stir in the crème de cassis. Keep the glaze warm while assembling the tart.

To assemble, spread the basil pastry cream evenly over the bottom of the prebaked tart shell. Arrange the raspberries close together, domed side up, over the pastry cream until they cover the pastry cream completely. Spoon or, with a small pastry brush, brush the warm currant glaze over the berries. Carefully remove the sides of the tart pan and with the help of a wide metal spatula, slide the tart off its metal disk onto a serving plate.

Note ■ The center of the tart can be garnished with a small sprig of basil, or sprigs of basil leaves can be placed around the rim of the serving plate. The tart is pretty enough by itself, however, to need no decoration. Of course, strawberries may be substituted for the raspberries. Leave them whole if they are small, or slice and arrange decoratively if they are large.

RED CABBAGE TART WITH GINGERED BROWN SUGAR PASTRY CREAM

Serves 6

*t*his is a rich, spicy tart assembled in a crunchy hazelnut tart shell. The hazelnuts or filberts (cultivated hazelnuts) are ground with their skins left on—for flavor, color, and texture. Skinning hazelnuts is time-consuming and a bore. There is nothing wrong with leaving the skins on (they're not bitter), except that they deepen the color of whatever you are making and, if not ground as they are here, they could add an unpleasant, papery texture. The red cabbage is cooked in a mixture that is akin to mulled wine, giving the vegetable a piquant-sweet taste that works in harmony with the gingered pastry cream and the nut crust.

HAZELNUT TART SHELL

- ¾ cup hazelnuts or filberts (cultivated hazelnuts), with skins
- 2 tablespoons granulated sugar
- 1¼ cups all-purpose flour
- ½ teaspoon salt, or to taste
- 6 tablespoons (¾ stick) cold unsalted butter, cut into bits
- 3 tablespoons ice water

TOPPING

- 1 cup dry red wine
- 1 cinnamon stick
- ½ teaspoon ground cloves
- 1 cup granulated sugar
- 1½ pounds red cabbage (1 small head), cored and finely shredded

PASTRY CREAM

- 3 large egg yolks, at room temperature
- ½ cup packed light brown sugar
- 3 tablespoons all-purpose flour
- ¼ cup milk, scalded
- 1 tablespoon unsalted butter
- ¼ teaspoon salt, or to taste
- 1 tablespoon grated peeled fresh gingerroot
- 1 teaspoon granulated sugar

To make the tart shell, coarsely grind the hazelnuts with the sugar in a food processor. Add the flour, salt, and butter and pulse the mixture until it resembles coarse meal. Transfer the mixture to a bowl, sprinkle it with 3 tablespoons ice water, and toss it with a fork until the water is completely incorporated and the mixture begins to form a thick paste. Press the dough into the bottom and up the sides of a 7½-inch fluted tart pan with a removable bottom, building up the sides and pressing the dough firmly into the flutings. Chill the shell for 30 minutes.

Preheat the oven to 425°F.

Line the pastry shell with a sheet of foil, and fill the foil with pie weights, raw rice, or dried beans. Bake the shell in the center of the oven for 7 minutes, remove the foil and weights, and bake the shell 5 minutes more, or until it is golden. Cool in the pan on a wire rack.

To make the cabbage topping, in a medium saucepan or sauté pan, combine the wine, cinnamon stick, ground cloves, and sugar and bring to a boil over moderately high heat, stirring until the sugar is dissolved. Add the cabbage and cook for 2 minutes, turn the heat down to simmer, and continue to cook, stirring occasionally, for 15 minutes more, or until the cabbage is just tender. Remove from the heat and let the cabbage cool in the syrup.

To make the pastry cream, in the bowl of an electric mixer set on medium speed, beat the egg yolks for 1 minute. Add the brown sugar a little at a time, beating, and beat the mixture until it falls in a ribbon when the beaters are lifted. Beat in the flour. Transfer the mixture to a heavy saucepan over moderately low heat and add the scalded milk in a stream, whisking constantly. Bring to a boil and, continuing to whisk, boil the mixture for 2 minutes. Whisk in the butter, salt, and the gingerroot, and remove from heat. Sprinkle the surface of the cream with the sugar to prevent a skin from forming (alternately, cover the surface with a piece of plastic wrap or a buttered round of wax paper) and let cool for 1 hour.

To assemble the tart, carefully remove the rim of the tart pan and with the help of a wide metal spatula, slide the shell off its metal disk and onto a serving plate. Stir the cooled pastry cream and spread it evenly over the bottom of the shell. With a slotted spoon, lift the cabbage from the pan, letting the syrup drain off (discard the syrup or save it for another use) before spreading it over the surface of the cream, mounding it slightly in the center. Serve in wedges at room temperature or partially chilled.

ELEGANT CARROT AND BROWN SUGAR TART

Serves 6 to 8

*a*s the saying goes, "You can never be too rich or too thin." This tart is both. The filling is only about a half-inch high, in the manner of great restaurant kitchens. A slice contains just enough pleasure to make your taste buds beg for more—sweet, creamy tasting, a mixture of euphoric delights.

Crunchy Pecan Crust (page 97)

2 cups half-and-half

¼ cup granulated sugar

1 tablespoon pure vanilla extract

¼ cup firmly packed light brown sugar

1 tablespoon unsalted butter

1 cup peeled and finely grated carrots

1 cup heavy (whipping) cream

Preheat the oven to 425°F.

Prepare the Crunchy Pecan Crust and press the dough into an 8½-inch fluted tart pan with a removable bottom. Continue to follow the directions for pricking, chilling, and prebaking the crust.

Reduce the oven to 375°F.

While the crust is baking, begin preparing the filling. In a medium saucepan, combine the half-and-half, granulated sugar, and vanilla and bring to a boil over moderate heat, whisking constantly. Boil for 1 minute, reduce the heat to a simmer, and cook, whisking occasionally, until reduced by one-third, about 20 minutes. Remove the saucepan from the heat and whisk in the light brown sugar and butter until well combined. Stir in the carrots and keep warm while the crust cools.

When the crust has cooled, place the tart pan on a cookie sheet and pour in the filling. Bake on the cookie sheet in the middle of the oven for 50 minutes, or until the center of the filling moves slightly when the tart pan is shaken. Cool on a wire rack to room temperature, or until the filling is completely set. The filling may pull away slightly from the edges of the crust. (The tart can be made up to 1 day in advance, covered, and refrigerated.) To remove the tart from the pan, place the tart pan on a small bowl and gently press down on the sides of the pan to release the tart. A thin, pointed knife may be needed to help free the crust from the pan. Transfer the tart on its metal disk to a serving plate or cake stand.

Beat the cream until stiff peaks form and spread it over the tart with a metal spatula, or serve the cream on the side. Serve the tart chilled or at room temperature.

RHUBARB STRAWBERRY NUT TART WITH CINNAMON CRUMB TOPPING

Serves 6 to 8

*r*hubarb is one of those members of the plant world, like tomatoes, whose use dictates its common classification. It is really a vegetable, but because most of us use it in sweet pies or stewed with fruit we consider it a fruit. We caution you to eat only the stalks. The leaves contain an as-yet-unidentified toxin which can be quite poisonous to some people. This recipe combines some of our favorite elements: the Brown Butter Sugar Crust, a cinnamon-flavored streusel topping, and the elusive touch of citrus.

1 unbaked deep-dish 9-inch Brown Butter Sugar Crust tart shell (page 114)

1 cup ground walnuts, hazelnuts, or pecans

1 cup granulated sugar

¼ cup all-purpose flour

1 tablespoon grated orange zest

2 cups rhubarb (about ¾ pound), cut into ½-inch pieces

2 cups (1 pint) whole small strawberries or halved larger strawberries

½ cup (1 stick) unsalted butter, softened

½ cup firmly packed dark brown sugar

1 teaspoon cinnamon

1 cup all-purpose flour

Preheat the oven to 400°F.

Prepare the tart shell according to the recipe. Distribute the nuts evenly over the bottom of the shell and press lightly into the pastry.

In a medium bowl, gently toss the sugar, flour, orange zest, rhubarb, and strawberries together. Fill the tart shell with the mixture.

To make the crumb topping, in a medium bowl cream together the butter and sugar with a wooden spoon. Sprinkle with the cinnamon and, with a fork, cut in the flour until the mixture resembles coarse meal. Distribute the crumb topping over the filled tart.

Place the tart on a cookie sheet and bake in the lower third of the oven for 50 to 60 minutes, or until the juices are bubbly and the crust is golden brown.

Note ■ You may eliminate the strawberries in the filling and double the amount of rhubarb.

BROWN BUTTER PIECRUST

Makes 1 piecrust

*U*sing brown butter in place of fresh sweet butter gives the standard pie dough or *pâte brisée* a nutty, richer, even more buttery taste. You must think ahead, however, because the butter not only needs to be browned but completely chilled as well to resolidify it. But the extra time and thought necessary is well worth it once you taste the result. It's a revelation. From then on we think that you, like us, will want to use this recipe for your standard (anything but!) crust.

6 tablespoons (¾ stick) unsalted butter	¼ teaspoon salt
1¼ cups all-purpose flour	3 tablespoons ice water
2 tablespoons cold solid vegetable shortening	

In a small saucepan or skillet over moderate heat, melt the butter and, watching carefully, cook it until it turns chestnut brown, about 5 minutes or more. Pour immediately into a ramekin or small heatproof bowl and resolidify in the refrigerator or freezer (this should be done 2 hours or up to 3 days ahead of time). Cut the solid browned butter into small pieces.

In a large chilled bowl, with a pastry blender or two knives, blend the flour, browned butter bits, shortening, and salt together until the mixture resembles coarse meal. Add the ice water all at once and toss the mixture with two forks until the water is incorporated. (You can do all this in a food processor, pulsing a few times to blend the ingredients. If you use a food processor, omit the next step.) Quickly form the dough into a ball and knead it several times (but don't overwork it or it will become tough when baked) on a flat surface to distribute the butter and shortening evenly. Reform into a ball (if using a food processor, form into a ball directly from the workbowl).

Dust the ball of dough with flour, flatten it slightly, wrap in wax paper, and chill for at least 1 hour (or up to 24 hours) before rolling.

To roll out the pastry, lightly flour a board, pastry cloth, or work surface. Lightly flour a rolling pin and press it down into the center of the dough ball. Roll gently away from you out toward the edge. Keep rolling gently from the center out to the edge, turning the dough little by little until you have shaped it evenly into a circle (or square or rectangle, as called for in the recipe) of the desired size and thickness. To transfer it into the pie pan, roll it over the rolling pin and transfer it to the pan, unrolling it evenly over the bottom or, alternately, fold the circle of dough in half and then in half again, place the point of the quarter circle at the center of the pan and unfold.

To partially bake a one-crust pie shell, preheat the oven to 425°F. for at least 15 minutes.

Roll out the dough ball to the size specified in the recipe and line the pie pan, pressing the dough lightly into the sides of the pan with the back of a teaspoon to fit the pastry snugly without stretching it. With a sharp knife or scissors, trim the overhanging pastry to about 1 inch beyond the rim of the pan, fold this back on itself, and crimp the double edge all around by pressing with the tines of a fork. To flute the edge, fold the trimmed overhanging dough under itself. Spread the thumb and forefinger of one hand about an inch apart, resting them lightly on the pastry rim. With the forefinger of the other hand, push against the pastry on the rim while you pinch the pastry with your other hand to form an upstanding fluted ridge. Move all around the rim of the pastry in the same way.

Before baking, lightly prick the bottom and sides of the pastry shell all over with a fork (try not to pierce the pastry all the way through or any liquid in the filling might seep through). Line with a sheet of wax paper and fit another pie pan of the same size inside the *crimped* pastry shell or alternately (and for a standing *fluted* pie shell) line the pastry shell with aluminum foil and fill with pie weights, raw rice, or dried beans. Bake the shell in the middle of the oven for 8 minutes, remove the inside pie pan or the foil and weights, and bake the pie shell for 5 minutes more, or until it is just beginning to turn golden. Cool the crust in the pan before filling.

For a fully prebaked one-crust pie shell, bake as above but after removing the inside pan or the aluminum foil and weights, reduce the oven heat to 400°F. and bake the pie shell for 8 to 10 minutes longer, or until it is golden brown. Cool the crust in the pan before filling. (The prebaked pie shell can be baked a day ahead and stored at room temperature—or up to 2 months ahead, frozen, and thawed for ½ hour before filling.)

Note ■ For a two-crust pie, simply double the above recipe but increase the ice water to just 4 tablespoons. If you feel you need a little more water, add it, but be very careful you don't add too much. The less water used the better. The pastry should stick together when you form it into a ball but not be doughy. Dust the ball of dough and refrigerate as above. When you are about to roll out the dough, cut it in half, keeping one-half chilled until you are ready to use it. Roll out both crusts in the same manner.

BROWN BUTTER SUGAR CRUST

Makes 1 tart shell

*t*he brown butter in this tart crust gives it a richer, nutty flavor that other tart crusts can't match. It's almost like a cookie dough, a wonderfully crisp, crunchy vessel to hold any sweet filling.

¾ cup (1½ sticks) unsalted butter

2 cups all-purpose flour

¼ cup granulated sugar

　Finely grated zest of 1 lemon

3 large hard-cooked egg yolks, chilled
　and mashed

2 large raw egg yolks, chilled

½ teaspoon salt

In a small saucepan or skillet over moderate heat, melt the butter and, watching carefully, cook for about 5 minutes, shaking the pan occasionally, until the butter turns chestnut brown. Pour immediately into a ramekin or small, heatproof bowl and resolidify in the refrigerator or freezer until very firm (this should be done at least 2 hours or up to 3 days ahead of time). Cut the solid browned butter into small pieces.

Place the flour in a large chilled bowl and make a well in the center. Place the rest of the ingredients in the well and, working quickly with your fingertips, make a paste of the ingredients in the well. Gradually rub the butter paste into the flour just until all the flour is incorporated and the mixture becomes a smooth, firm ball of dough. Wrap the dough ball in plastic wrap and refrigerate at least 1 hour or up to 24 hours (let it rest at room temperature after chilling until you can just about press your finger into it).

Roll the dough between two sheets of wax paper, rolling gently from the center out to the edge of the dough. Turn the dough little by little, loosening the wax paper occasionally to allow the dough to spread, until you have rolled the dough evenly into a circle, square, or rectangle 1 inch larger than the tart or pie pan. Peel off the top sheet of wax paper, slip your hand under the bottom sheet, and invert the paper and pastry over the tart pan, centering it. Carefully peel off the paper and let the pastry fall slackly into the pan. Now gently press the pastry into the sides of the tart or pie pan. If using a fluted pan, carefully press the pastry into the flutings until it fits snugly, then run the rolling pin over the rim of the pan to cut away excess pastry, leaving a flush edge. If the pastry has been placed in a pie pan, run the back of a teaspoon around the sides of the pan to fit the pastry snugly without stretching it, then cut away the overhanging pastry to within 1 inch of the edge of the pan and fold it under itself to make a thick edge which can be fluted (see directions for a partially baked pie shell, page 113) or crimped all around with the tines of a fork.

Incidentally, keep the scraps and trimmings of pastry and freeze them, well wrapped, for making small tarts, lattice tops, or small decorative shapes to ornament tarts (cut them out and bake them on a cookie sheet until they are just golden and crisp, then position them on the finished tart).

To partially bake an unfilled sugar crust chill the pastry well, preferably in the freezer before baking. Preheat the oven to 350°F. Transfer the chilled pastry shell directly from the refrigerator or freezer to the center rack of the oven. Prick the bottom all over with the tines of a fork, line the shell with aluminum foil, and fill it with pie weights, raw rice, or dried beans. Bake for 10 minutes, lift out the aluminum foil with the weights, and continue baking for 5 minutes more, or until just beginning to turn golden.

To fully prebake an unfilled sugar crust, follow the procedure for the partially baked crust, but after removing the foil and weights, continue baking for 15 minutes more, or until golden brown all over.

PUDDINGS, CUSTARDS, SOUFFLÉS, AND MOUSSES

We love puddings and all their relatives. We love the textures that are created in the cooking—some spongy, some smooth and creamy, some light and airy, others cakelike—all so satisfying.

Actually, the steamed pudding was the forerunner of the cake. Before temperature-regulated ovens came into existence, steaming offered the cook a fail-safe, constant cooking temperature.

Some of the desserts in this section are made on top of the stove while others go into the oven. Some are served hot, some cold, some at room temperature. There's a recipe for every season and every taste. There is even a zabaglione made with a vegetable liqueur, Cynar, an Italian invention distilled from artichokes. It has a light, bittersweet flavor that can become addictive.

Carrot Custard Pudding with Pistachios ■ *Gingered Three-Tiered Sponge Pudding* ■ *Baked Parsnip Pudding with Hot Lemon Sauce* ■ *Zucchini Ginger Steamed Pudding* ■ *Fennel Bread Pudding with Caramel Espresso Sauce* ■ *Zucchini Orange Pudding in Its Own Caramel Sauce* ■ *Pois Chiches Glacés Chocolate Pots de Crème* ■ *Zuppa Italiano con Finocchio, Ceci, Cioccolata e Caffè, or Tiramisu with Fennel* ■ *Artichoke Zabaglione* ■ *Baked Pumpkin Custard* ■ *Sweet Angel Artichoke Soufflé* ■ *Warm Pink Bean Mexican Cream* ■ *Baked Basil Cream Soufflés over Bittersweet Chocolate Mousse*

CARROT CUSTARD PUDDING
WITH PISTACHIOS

Serves 4 to 6

*i*n many kitchens the only time pistachios appear is peeking out from slices of pâté. We like them for their pale green color, as well as their flavor and texture. In this dessert they add chewiness to an otherwise creamy smooth pudding; their pastel color is a welcome contrast to the orange tint imparted by the carrots.

10 tablespoons (1¼ sticks) unsalted butter, at room temperature	2 tablespoons grated orange zest
1 cup firmly packed light brown sugar	1 teaspoon grated lemon zest
2 large eggs, lightly beaten, at room temperature	½ teaspoon powdered ginger
	½ teaspoon mace
2 cups peeled and grated raw carrots	½ teaspoon allspice
¾ cup crushed vanilla wafers	¾ cup shelled unsalted whole pistachios

Preheat the oven to 350°F.

Generously butter a 6-cup baking dish and set aside.

In the large bowl of an electric mixer set at medium speed, cream together the butter and sugar until well blended. Add the eggs and carrots and continue to beat 2 minutes longer. Add the vanilla wafers, orange and lemon zest, ginger, mace, and allspice and beat well, about 2 minutes more.

With a rubber spatula, fold in ½ cup pistachios. Pour the batter into the prepared baking dish and bake in the center of the oven for 1 hour.

Meanwhile, chop the remaining pistachios in a food processor, with a nut grinder, or by hand.

When the custard is finished baking, remove it from the oven and, while still hot, sprinkle the top with the chopped pistachios. Serve from the baking dish either warm, at room temperature, or chilled.

GINGERED THREE-TIERED SPONGE PUDDING

Serves 6

*W*e love baked puddings, especially ones like this, which separates into three distinctively textured layers as it bakes. When it is inverted onto a serving plate the bottom is a chewy meringue crust, the center is soft and spongy like a cake, and the top is creamy and light, almost a sauce. It can be garnished with chopped crystallized ginger, shavings of bittersweet chocolate, or sprinkled with chocolate cookie crumbs. We suggest that it be served chilled, but it is equally good warm or at room temperature.

2 tablespoons peeled and minced fresh gingerroot	**¼** cup all-purpose flour
½ cup Stone's Ginger Wine (available at most good liquor stores)	**1½** cups milk
2 tablespoons unsalted butter, at room temperature	Pinch of salt
¾ cup plus 5 tablespoons superfine sugar	Chopped crystallized ginger, chopped or shaved bittersweet chocolate, or chocolate cookie or cake crumbs for garnish
4 large eggs, separated, at room temperature	

Preheat the oven to 350°F.

Butter six 1-cup ovenproof glass custard cups.

In a small bowl, combine the gingerroot and ginger wine and set aside. In the bowl of an electric mixer set at medium speed, cream the butter with ¾ cup sugar for 1 minute, or until light and lemony colored. Add the egg yolks one at a time, beating well after each addition. Beat in half the flour until combined, then beat in the reserved ginger wine mixture until blended. Beat in the remaining flour and the milk until thoroughly combined and set aside.

In another bowl of the electric mixer set at medium speed, using clean beaters, beat the egg whites until foamy. Add the salt and continue beating until the whites hold soft peaks. Beat in the remaining 5 tablespoons sugar, 1 tablespoon at a time, until completely incorporated and the whites hold stiff peaks. With a rubber spatula, gently fold the whites into the ginger mixture until completely blended. Transfer the mixture equally into the custard cups. Place the cups in a roasting pan and set the pan in the middle of the oven. Pour warm water into the pan to halfway up the sides of the cups.

Bake for about 35 minutes, or until the puddings puff up and brown and a cake tester inserted near the edge comes out clean. Remove the cups from the water bath and set on a rack to cool to room temperature. The puddings will crack and sink as they cool. Cover the puddings with plastic wrap or foil and refrigerate for 2 hours or overnight.

To unmold, run the tip of a small, sharp knife around the edge of each pudding to help release it. Invert onto individual dessert plates and release by warming each custard cup with a hair dryer or hot damp tea towel for several seconds before lifting it from the pudding. Decorate the puddings with the garnish of your choice.

Alternatively, cool the puddings on the rack until they are warm or at room temperature. Run the tip of a knife around the edge of each pudding, unmold onto a dessert plate, and garnish.

BAKED PARSNIP PUDDING WITH HOT LEMON SAUCE

Serves 6 to 8

*P*umpkin, a vegetable unknown in Europe before the seventeenth century, was introduced by Native Americans to the first colonists in Massachusetts. They turned it into a dessert ingredient soon after. It was not distasteful to these early residents to utilize other vegetables in sweet mixtures as well. Carrots and parsnips soon followed pumpkin and the already popular corn as ingredients in such things as carrot pudding and parsnip pie. Recipes like this one found their way into cookbooks, but not until the early 1900s. Inventive cooks very likely used them as guides for today's carrot cakes, which have become standards.

½ cup (1 stick) unsalted butter

½ cup firmly packed dark brown sugar

1 large egg, at room temperature

1 cup peeled and grated raw parsnips (about 2 medium)

2 teaspoons grated lemon zest

1 cup golden raisins

1¼ cups all-purpose flour

1 teaspoon baking powder

Pinch of salt

½ teaspoon freshly grated nutmeg

½ teaspoon cinnamon

½ teaspoon baking soda

1 tablespoon hot water

Hot Lemon Sauce (recipe follows)

Preheat the oven to 350°F.

Butter a 4-cup tube-type mold.

In the bowl of an electric mixer set on medium speed, cream the butter with the brown sugar until light and fluffy. Add the egg and beat until smooth. Add all of the remaining ingredients and continue to beat until well combined. Pour the mixture into the mold and bake in the center of the oven for about 50 minutes, or until a tester comes out clean. Let cool in the pan on a wire rack for 10 minutes. Run a sharp knife around the edge of the pudding and invert onto a serving platter. Serve warm or at room temperature with lemon sauce, whipped cream, heavy cream, or vanilla ice cream.

HOT LEMON SAUCE

Makes 2 cups

½ cup freshly squeezed lemon juice

1¾ cups water

1 cup firmly packed light or dark
brown sugar

¼ cup granulated sugar

4 tablespoons (½ stick) unsalted
butter

⅛ teaspoon salt, or to taste

2 tablespoons cornstarch

In a medium saucepan over moderately high heat, combine the lemon juice, 1½ cups water, the sugars, butter, and salt. Bring to a boil and cook 2 minutes, stirring constantly with a wire whisk.

Meanwhile, mix the cornstarch and remaining ¼ cup water together until smooth. Whisk into the boiling mixture and cook, stirring constantly, until smooth and thickened. Serve hot.

Note ■ The sauce may be made ahead and reheated over very low heat or in a double boiler over simmering water.

ZUCCHINI GINGER STEAMED PUDDING

Serves 6

S teamed puddings are very old-fashioned, very English, very good. They have been out of favor for decades, perhaps because they are slow to cook. That's a shame because they're easy to make and don't require the precise chemistry integral to the baking process. They can be made well ahead of time and stay warm for hours if left in the mold. You can even improvise with steamed puddings, make mistakes, and no one will be the wiser. The result is always a warm, moist, cakelike dessert that's earthy and robust yet elegant—especially when served with clouds of whipped cream, ice cream, or a custard sauce. The texture of this pudding is dense, spongy, and full of the good tastes of ginger, cinnamon, brown sugar, and nuts. Because they are substantial, cook for a long time, and often heat up the kitchen, steamed puddings are usually served in autumn and winter. However, if you've ever tasted leftovers cold from the refrigerator or at room temperature, you realize at once that there is no reason to keep them strictly seasonal.

1 cup all-purpose flour	1 cup grated unpeeled zucchini (2 small, about ½ pound)
½ teaspoon baking soda	
2 tablespoons cinnamon	½ cup chopped crystallized ginger
½ cup (1 stick) unsalted butter, softened	½ cup coarsely chopped walnuts
	Vanilla Custard Sauce (optional, recipe follows)
½ cup firmly packed dark brown sugar	
2 large eggs, at room temperature	

Butter a 4-cup pudding mold with a lid (or any 4-cup decorative mold to be covered with a double layer of aluminum foil tied with a string). Set aside.

Sift together the flour, baking soda, and cinnamon and set aside.

In the bowl of an electric mixer, cream the butter and sugar at medium speed until smooth, about 2 to 3 minutes. Still at medium speed, add the eggs one at a time, beating well after each addition. On low speed, fold in the sifted dry ingredients until incorporated; then fold in the zucchini, ginger, and walnuts, mixing until thoroughly combined. Pour into the prepared mold, cover the mold securely (with its lid or with the double layer of aluminum foil tied tightly with string below the lip of the mold), and set into a larger kettle on a steaming rack (or set into a steamer). Pour boiling water into the kettle to reach halfway up the sides of the mold. Cover the kettle and simmer over moderately low heat for 2 hours, checking occasionally and adding more boiling water if necessary. Transfer the mold to a rack (it will stay warm in the covered mold for several hours) to cool slightly.

Just before serving, unmold onto a serving platter. Serve in wedges topped with vanilla-flavored whipped cream, scoops of vanilla ice cream, or Vanilla Custard Sauce.

VANILLA CUSTARD SAUCE

Makes about 1½ cups

1 cup confectioners' sugar	1 large egg, beaten
½ cup (1 stick) unsalted butter, softened	Pinch of salt
	1 teaspoon pure vanilla extract

In the top of a double boiler over barely simmering water or in a small, heavy saucepan over very low heat, whisk together the sugar and the butter until well combined. Continue to whisk while adding the beaten egg and salt and cook, whisking constantly, for about 5 minutes, or until the sauce is light and foamy. Add the vanilla and whisk until well combined. Serve warm or slightly chilled.

FENNEL BREAD PUDDING WITH CARAMEL ESPRESSO SAUCE

Serves 8

*W*e love bread pudding. It's a simple, down-home dessert that shines even at the most elegant dinner party. Fennel gives this rich version a subtle licorice flavor that melds beautifully with the coffee-tinged caramel sauce.

2 tablespoons unsalted butter	4 cups milk
1 fennel bulb (about 1 pound), trimmed and cut into ¼-inch dice plus 2 tablespoons minced green feathery fronds	1 tablespoon pure vanilla extract
	3 large eggs, at room temperature
	3 large egg yolks, at room temperature
1 teaspoon fennel seeds, lightly crushed in a mortar and pestle	1 cup heavy (whipping) cream
	¼ cup Sambuca, Pernod, anisette, or other licorice-flavored liqueur
¾ cup plus 1 tablespoon granulated sugar	¼ cup confectioners' sugar
1 long loaf French or Italian bread	Caramel Espresso Sauce (recipe follows)
⅓ cup melted unsalted butter	

Preheat the oven to 375°F.

In a skillet or small sauté pan set over moderate heat, melt the 2 tablespoons of butter. When the foam subsides, stir in the fennel and fennel seeds and sauté, stirring occasionally, until the fennel is softened, about 5 minutes. Add 1 tablespoon sugar and the feathery fronds, stir to combine, and set aside.

Cut the bread on the diagonal into ¼-inch-thick slices. Brush one side of each slice with the melted butter, place on a cookie sheet, buttered side up, and toast in the oven until crisp and golden brown, about 5 minutes. Turn the slices and toast the second side, watching the bread carefully so that it does not burn. Arrange the toast, the slices slightly overlapping, in the bottom of a 2-quart baking dish or oval gratin dish 1½ inches deep. Spread the sautéed fennel mixture evenly over the toast. Set aside.

In a medium saucepan, bring the milk and remaining ¾ cup sugar to a boil over moderately high heat, stirring, until the sugar is dissolved. Stir in the vanilla and remove from the heat.

In a small bowl, beat the whole eggs with the yolks and stir in the cream and Sambuca until well combined. Pour the egg mixture into the milk mixture in a thin stream, stirring constantly.

Strain the milk and egg mixture through a sieve evenly over the toast and fennel. Place the baking dish in a larger pan and transfer both to the bottom rack of the oven. Pour hot but not boiling water into the larger pan until it comes halfway up the sides of the baking dish and bake until the custard is set, about 35 to 45 minutes. To test for doneness, insert a knife into the center of the custard. If it comes out clean, the custard is done.

Remove the baking dish from the pan of water and sift the confectioners' sugar over the top of the pudding. Place under the broiler for 1 or 2 minutes to glaze lightly. Serve immediately, passing a sauceboat or a bowl of warm Caramel Espresso Sauce at the table.

CARAMEL ESPRESSO SAUCE

Makes about 1 cup

1 cup granulated sugar
½ cup water

½ cup hot strong brewed espresso

In a small saucepan, combine the sugar and the water and bring to a boil over moderately high heat. Continue cooking until the sugar starts to turn golden. Reduce the heat to moderate and continue cooking, watching carefully, until the syrup turns a dark walnut brown. Immediately remove the syrup from the heat and carefully add the espresso in a slow stream. (Adding liquid to the hot syrup can cause it to boil up and spatter.) Return to the heat and cook, stirring, until the sauce is thin and smooth.

ZUCCHINI ORANGE PUDDING IN ITS OWN CARAMEL SAUCE

Serves 6 to 8

*O*range and zucchini seem to be made for each other in this pudding. Chilling it overnight in the refrigerator creates more caramel sauce. However, most of the caramel clings to the pudding, so the ends become the most desirable servings. To create four end servings instead of two, slice the unmolded loaf down the center first before cutting individual pieces. When you have kids to satisfy, you must learn these little tricks to keep the peace.

½ cup granulated sugar

¼ cup freshly squeezed orange juice

½ cup all-purpose flour

1 cup confectioners' sugar

3 large eggs, separated

4 tablespoons (½ stick) unsalted butter, melted

1½ pounds zucchini, finely chopped in a blender or food processor

Grated zest of 1 orange

Preheat the oven to 350°F.

In a small saucepan, combine the granulated sugar with the orange juice and cook gently over moderately low heat, stirring occasionally, until the sugar has dissolved. Turn the heat up to moderately high and bring the sugar mixture to a boil without stirring, then boil rapidly until the syrup turns golden brown. Pour immediately into a 9 × 5 × 3-inch loaf pan (the pan gets hot, so hold it with an oven mitt or pot holder) and tilt the pan from side to side to coat the base and 1 inch up the sides with the caramel syrup. Set aside.

Sift the flour and confectioners' sugar into a large bowl. Make a well in the center and add the egg yolks, melted butter, zucchini, and orange zest. With a wire whisk, beat in the flour and sugar, pulling it little by little from the sides of the bowl until a smooth batter forms. With an electric mixer or whisk, beat the egg whites until stiff peaks form and carefully fold them into the zucchini mixture. Pour and scrape into the caramel-lined loaf pan and bake in the center of the oven for 1 hour, or until firm and golden brown on top. Set on a wire rack and cool to room temperature. To unmold, run a thin, sharp knife around the edge and invert onto a serving platter. Pour any caramel sauce in the pan around the sides or over the top of the pudding. Chill for 2 hours or up to 24 hours before serving.

POIS CHICHES GLACÉS CHOCOLATE POTS DE CRÈME

Serves 8

*O*ur favorite mousse is a deep, dark, almost bitter chocolate one. There is no heavy cream in the mousse, only eggs. The addition of pureed Pois Chiches Glacés (candied chickpeas) adds texture and a chestnutlike flavor that makes this dessert more complex and luxurious; that the chickpeas *(pois chiches)* also add protein, vitamins, and fiber is further justification. We always present it in white Ginori pots de crème cups, an anniversary present from Sally's sister Edy and her husband, Joe. Because these pots de crème have covers, we serve the whipped cream on the side.

½ cup Pois Chiches Glacés (page 173), with just the syrup that clings to them

½ pound best-quality bittersweet chocolate, finely chopped

5 tablespoons strong coffee or espresso

5 large eggs, separated, at room temperature

2 teaspoons dark rum, cognac, or Kahlúa

1 cup heavy (whipping) cream

In a small heavy saucepan, cook the Pois Chiches Glacés with their syrup, the chocolate, and the coffee over moderate heat, stirring occasionally, until the chocolate melts. Transfer to the bowl of a food processor, add the egg yolks and rum, and puree until smooth. Pour and scrape the puree into a bowl.

With an electric mixer or a wire whisk, beat the egg whites until stiff peaks form. Whisk one-fourth of the whites thoroughly into the puree to lighten it. Then, with a rubber spatula, fold in the remaining whites gently and thoroughly until no flecks of white remain. Fill each of the pots de crème or eight 6-ounce ramekins and refrigerate, covered, for at least 4 and up to 24 hours. Serve the pots de crème chilled with whipped cream on the side or mound the whipped cream in the ramekins.

ZUPPA ITALIANO CON FINOCCHIO, CECI, CIOCCOLATA E CAFFÈ, OR TIRAMISU WITH FENNEL

Serves 6 to 8

*t*iramisu, Venice's favorite dessert, has become so pervasive in Italian restaurants here that it is almost a cliché. There's nothing wrong with that—so is chocolate ice cream. We just thought it might be due for a little jolt of something to take it in another direction. What resulted was the addition of a layer of fennel puree. We spread the fennel puree not on the *savoiardi*, the ladyfingers Italians use, but on our Basic Chickpea Flourless Cake. Now we have created a dessert with two vegetables instead of one. What a great way to get two-thirds of your minimum daily requirement of vegetables!

1 fennel bulb (about 1 pound), trimmed and cut into ¼-inch dice plus 2 tablespoons minced green, feathery fronds

1 teaspoon fennel seeds

½ cup plus 4 tablespoons granulated sugar

½ cup water

1 Basic Chickpea Flourless Cake (page 20)

1 pound mascarpone (Italian triple-cream cheese available at Italian markets and most specialty food stores)

3 large eggs, separated, at room temperature

3 ounces best-quality bittersweet chocolate, grated

1 cup strong brewed espresso coffee, at room temperature

3 tablespoons coffee liqueur or brandy

¼ cup unsweetened cocoa powder, preferably Dutch process

In a medium saucepan set over moderately high heat, stir together the fennel (reserve the fronds), fennel seeds, 2 tablespoons sugar, and the water and bring to a boil. Reduce heat to simmer and cook, uncovered, about 15 minutes, or until tender and almost all the water has been reduced to a syrup. Transfer the fennel and its syrup to a food processor and pulse several times until it becomes a smooth puree. Transfer to a small bowl and stir in the minced fennel fronds. Set aside to cool completely.

Divide the cake into 2 layers. Set aside.

In a medium bowl, cream the mascarpone with a wooden spoon until smooth. Add the egg yolks and ½ cup sugar and continue stirring until well combined and very smooth. Stir in the grated chocolate.

In the bowl of an electric mixer or with a hand mixer on moderately high speed, beat the egg whites until stiff peaks form. With a spatula, fold one-fourth of the whites into the mascarpone mixture to lighten it, then gently but thoroughly fold in the remaining whites.

Place one cake layer, cut side up, on a round cake platter with a raised lip. Combine the coffee with the 2 remaining tablespoons sugar and the coffee liqueur, stirring until the sugar dissolves. Moisten the cake layer thoroughly by pouring or brushing ½ cup coffee mixture over it. Spread the layer with half of the reserved fennel puree, then half of the mascarpone mixture. Place the second cake layer, cut side up, over the first, moisten it with the remaining coffee, spread it with the remaining fennel puree, and end with the mascarpone mixture spread smoothly and evenly. Sift the cocoa powder over the top and refrigerate, covered loosely with plastic wrap, for 24 hours while the flavors meld. Remove from the refrigerator ½ hour before serving.

Note ■ If mascarpone is unavailable in your area, blend 1 cup heavy cream with ½ pound ricotta cheese in a blender or food processor until smooth and lump-free. Refrigerate until ready to use.

ARTICHOKE ZABAGLIONE

Serves 6

*i*taly's justly famous dessert foam is usually made with Marsala wine. Never satisfied with the usual, we tried it with a somewhat obscure Italian artichoke liqueur, Cynar. The flavor is as ethereal as the texture of zabaglione is gossamer. To achieve this texture, zabaglione must be cooked in a double boiler, or at least a heavy saucepan or heatproof mixing bowl held over barely simmering water in another pot. It also requires constant beating. We have found a hand beater to be less exhausting than a wire whisk and the results almost indistinguishable. Zabaglione is usually spooned into champagne flutes and served warm. But any large stemmed glass or glass dessert plates will do. We also like to serve it as a sauce over frozen or chilled desserts that call for a whipped cream topping. It's especially good with dark, bittersweet chocolate mousse.

6 large egg yolks, at room
   temperature
⅓ cup granulated sugar

⅔ cup Cynar (Italian artichoke liqueur,
   available at most well-stocked
   liquor stores)

In the bottom half of a double boiler over moderately low heat, bring an inch of water barely to a simmer.

In the top of the double boiler, off the heat, beat together the egg yolks and sugar with a hand mixer on medium-high speed until the sugar is dissolved and the mixture is light, creamy, and pale yellow, about 3 to 5 minutes. Place the pot with the yolk mixture into the bottom of the double boiler and add the Cynar a little at a time, beating constantly. As it heats, the beaten mixture will begin to foam and double in volume. Continue beating until it thickens and forms soft peaks that barely hold their shape, about 7 to 10 minutes. Spoon the foam into champagne flutes, goblets, or glass dessert bowls and serve immediately.

Note ■ To serve as a sauce, transfer the zabaglione to a sauceboat and serve warm in generous dollops over mousse, pumpkin pie, fruit tarts, steamed or baked puddings, and cakes.

Variations ■ For Cold Zabaglione Cream Dessert, let the foam cool completely and fold in 1 cup heavy whipping cream, unsweetened, whipped to stiff peaks. Chill in individual glass bowls and serve with plain cookies or plain pound cake. The increased volume will stretch this version to serve 8 or more.

For Zabaglione Gelato, Italian ice cream, cool the foam and combine it with 1½ cups heavy whipping cream whipped to the consistency of thick sour cream (making about 2½ cups), pour into an electric ice cream maker, and proceed to freeze according to the manufacturer's instructions.

BAKED PUMPKIN CUSTARD

Serves 6 to 8

*a*merican Indians ate the big yellow squash—the pumpkin. The first colonists knew a good thing when they saw it. Soon pumpkin was being cooked on their hearths, pureed and blended with a basic custard mixture and spices to become the forerunner of today's pumpkin pie. You can substitute acorn squash, patty pan, summer squash, or any of your other favorites for the pumpkin. The color of the filling may change accordingly, but the taste and texture will vary only slightly.

2 cups milk or half-and-half	½ teaspoon cinnamon
1 teaspoon unsalted butter, softened	½ teaspoon freshly grated nutmeg
3 large eggs, beaten	½ teaspoon powdered ginger
½ cup firmly packed light brown sugar	1 cup home-cooked or canned pureed
½ teaspoon salt, or to taste	pumpkin

Preheat the oven to 350°F.

In a medium saucepan over moderately high heat, scald the milk or half-and-half. Remove from the heat and whisk in the butter, eggs, sugar, salt, cinnamon, nutmeg, ginger, and pumpkin. Pour into a shallow 1-quart baking dish or into six 6-ounce custard cups. Set the filled baking dish or cups into a larger pan and pour in hot water to a depth of about 1 inch. Bake 40 to 45 minutes, or until a knife inserted in the center comes out clean. Serve warm or chilled.

Note ■ Pumpkin custard takes to embellishments like toasted chopped walnuts or pecans or a heavy sprinkling of brown sugar brought to bubbling under the broiler.

SWEET ANGEL ARTICHOKE SOUFFLÉ

Serves 6

•

*i*f you, your family, or guests restrict cholesterol intake (and, of course, we all should), this egg yolk–free soufflé is the perfect solution to the problem of what to serve for dessert—and we defy anyone to feel deprived! Artichoke soufflés can taste even sweeter after the first bite because artichokes contain a substance that intensifies the sweetness of other foods.

1 cup water	2 tablespoons fresh lemon juice
1 9-ounce package frozen artichoke hearts	6 egg whites, at room temperature
1 cup superfine sugar	¾ cup finely ground toasted, unsalted cashews or blanched almonds
½ cup Cynar (Italian artichoke liqueur)	

Oil and sugar a 2-quart soufflé dish, tapping out any excess sugar. Oil a 6-inch-wide doubled piece of foil or wax paper long enough to fit around the dish. Secure the collar with string so that it extends 2 inches above the rim. Set aside.

In a small saucepan, bring the water to a boil over moderately high heat. Add the artichokes and return to a boil, then reduce the heat to a simmer and cook the artichokes for 5 minutes. In the food processor, puree the artichokes with their liquid. Transfer the puree to a bowl and stir in ¾ cup sugar, the Cynar, and the lemon juice; combine well and let cool. (The puree may be prepared in advance up to this point, covered tightly with plastic wrap, and refrigerated for up to 3 hours. Return to room temperature before continuing.)

Preheat the oven to 375°F.

In the bowl of an electric mixer set on high speed, beat the egg whites until frothy. Add the remaining ¼ cup sugar, a little at a time, and beat until the whites hold stiff peaks. Stir one-quarter of the whites into the artichoke puree, then fold the lightened puree into the remaining whites gently but thoroughly. Fold in the cashews. Spoon the mixture into the prepared dish and bake the soufflé in the center of the oven for 30 to 35 minutes, or until the top is puffed and golden. Remove the collar and serve immediately plain, with sweetened and Cynar-flavored whipped cream, or with warm Brandied Apricot Syrup (see page 145).

Note ■ A collar is not necessary to make the soufflé rise, but it does give the egg whites a lot more confidence. If you're secure enough to let them go it on their own, please do. Another thought: if you like the finished soufflé to have a "top hat," run a thin-bladed knife in a 3-inch circle around the center of the soufflé batter before baking.

WARM PINK BEAN MEXICAN CREAM

Serves 8

*t*his is a south-of-the-border version of crème brûlée—in a way. It uses no heavy cream, no vanilla bean, and no brown sugar. And it's pink, not white. What's the similarity, then, you might ask, and we'd be hard put for an answer except that the custard is topped with sugar and broiled before serving. The main similarity, though, is that it too is elegant, creamy, and delicious.

1 cup pink bean puree, made from unseasoned home-cooked or canned pink beans (rinsed and drained)
1 quart milk
1 cup plus 8 teaspoons granulated sugar

Zest of 1 lemon pared in a strip with a swivel-bladed vegetable peeler
1 3-inch cinnamon stick
9 large egg yolks
5 tablespoons cornstarch
8 teaspoons cinnamon sugar, or more to taste

In a heavy medium saucepan, whisk together the bean puree with 3 cups milk and the sugar. Add the lemon zest and cinnamon stick. Stir and set aside.

In a bowl, whisk together the egg yolks, the cornstarch, and the remaining cup milk. Pour the mixture through a sieve into the bean mixture, set over high heat, and bring to a boil. Reduce the heat to simmer and cook, stirring constantly with a wooden spoon, until it starts to thicken. Simmer, stirring, 2 minutes more, or until smooth and quite thick. Pick out and discard the cinnamon stick and lemon zest.

Divide the custard among 8 heatproof 1-cup custard cups and sprinkle the top of each with 1 of the 8 teaspoons of cinnamon sugar. Set the cups in a baking pan and broil about 4 inches from the heat for about 2 minutes, or until the sugar caramelizes. Watch carefully to prevent the sugar from burning. Serve warm or refrigerate for 1 hour or overnight and serve cold.

BAKED BASIL CREAM SOUFFLÉS OVER BITTERSWEET CHOCOLATE MOUSSE

Serves 4

*d*on't let the length of this recipe deter you. It takes a long time to explain but it really is very easy. And besides, you can make its parts a day ahead—then put it together and bake it just before serving. We've made this dessert with fresh mint leaves which, to us, taste very much like basil. But basil also offers a grace note of anise, making it a much more complex flavoring than mint and subtler, as well. You can buy fresh basil all year long these days so you needn't wait until summer to serve these soufflés, a boon since they taste and look best right from the oven.

BASIL CREAM

1 cup milk	½ cup granulated sugar
½ cup firmly packed chopped fresh basil leaves	2½ tablespoons all-purpose flour
2 large egg yolks, at room temperature	

CHOCOLATE MOUSSE

½ cup heavy (whipping) cream	3 ounces best-quality bittersweet chocolate, finely chopped

SOUFFLÉ

3 large egg whites, at room temperature	¼ cup granulated sugar

Unsweetened cocoa powder for garnish	4 basil sprigs for garnish

To make the basil cream, in a small, heavy saucepan, scald the milk over moderately high heat. Remove the pan from the heat and stir in the basil. Let the mixture stand for at least 5 minutes to develop flavor. Pour the mixture through a fine metal sieve into a small bowl or measuring cup, pressing hard on the basil to extract as much of its essence as possible. In a medium bowl, whisk the egg yolks with the sugar until the mixture is thoroughly blended; sift the flour over the mixture, and whisk the mixture until well combined. Add the basil-flavored milk in a slow stream, whisking until incorporated. In a heavy saucepan, bring the mixture to a boil over moderately high heat, whisking, and boil it, whisking, for 1 minute. Transfer the basil cream to a bowl, cover tightly with plastic wrap, and set aside to cool (this can be made up to a day in advance, covered, and refrigerated).

To make the chocolate mousse, in a small heavy saucepan over moderately high heat, bring ¼ cup heavy cream just to a boil. Remove the pan from the heat and stir in the chocolate until it is melted and the mixture is smooth. Cover tightly with plastic wrap and set aside to cool to room temperature. In a chilled bowl with an electric mixer or hand mixer, beat the remaining ¼ cup heavy cream until it holds soft peaks. Stir one-third of the whipped cream into the cooled chocolate mixture, then fold in the remaining whipped cream gently but thoroughly (this can be made up to a day in advance, covered, and refrigerated).

Preheat the oven to 400°F.

Divide the chocolate mousse equally between 4 lightly buttered 4-inch ramekins or soufflé dishes 1½ inches deep, spreading it evenly.

When the basil cream has cooled to room temperature (or, if chilled, brought to room temperature), make the soufflé. In a bowl with an electric mixer or hand mixer, beat the egg whites until they are frothy. Add the ¼ cup sugar gradually, beating the whites until they hold stiff peaks. Stir one-third of the whites into the basil cream, then fold in the remaining whites gently but thoroughly.

Divide the basil cream soufflé mixture evenly between the 4 ramekins of chocolate mousse, spreading and mounding it so that it covers and seals the mousse completely. Place the ramekins on a cookie sheet and bake the soufflés in the middle of the oven for 15 minutes, or until puffed and golden.

Sift the cocoa over the soufflés, top with the basil sprigs, and serve immediately.

Note ■ Although the soufflés are best served hot, they may be held for up to 3 hours and served at room temperature. As they cool, however, the soufflés will deflate slightly. They may look a little wilted, but nothing can flatten that flavor! Even the most avid basil enthusiasts, when asked to identify what is flavoring the soufflé, are stumped.

CREPES, DUMPLINGS, AND OTHER SWEET DELIGHTS

What we offer here are flavor combinations, cooking techniques, and textures beyond the predictable. There are new minglings and pairings that will thrill your palate and your eye.

Mocha Risotto is a dessert fancier's dream: rich and chocolately with the smoothness of mascarpone cheese. And our faux marrons glacés are delicious (and inexpensive) stand-ins for the real thing in the impressive French treat, Mont Blanc.

Perhaps we shouldn't play favorites, however. We think you'll discover that all the desserts in this section are quite special, pleasing, and surprising.

Squash Flower Tempura with Cocoa Sugar ■ *Puffed Pumpkin*

Crepes with Cinnamon Sugar and Sour Cream ■ *Chocolate-Stuffed*

Potato Dumplings with Brandied Apricot Syrup ■ *Plum-Stuffed*

Mashed Potato Dumplings in Cinnamon Toast Crumbs ■

Rosemary-Scented Sweet Italian Flat Bread ■ *Corn Kernel Shortcakes*

with Berries 'n Cream ■ *Apricot Risotto* ■ *Mocha Risotto* ■ *Mont*

Blanc, or Pois Chiches Glacés Snow-Capped Mountain ■ *Jicama*

Honey Fool Spiked with Sage

SQUASH FLOWER TEMPURA WITH COCOA SUGAR

Makes 24 tempura flowers serving 4 to 6

*a*lthough fried, this is a light dessert. It can be accompanied by ice cream or stand alone. Either way it is unusual and, if your zucchini crop is abundant (and that's the only way they grow, it seems), this is yet another way to use up the harvest. If you're city dwellers, as we are, you can often find squash flowers at farmers' markets, Italian markets, and specialty produce stores. Buy a few extra to place, uncooked, in the center of the serving plate.

4 large eggs, separated	24 squash flowers, washed gently and patted dry
2 cups all-purpose flour	1 rounded tablespoon cocoa powder
2 cups Sauternes or other sweet white dessert wine	2 rounded tablespoons granulated or superfine sugar
⅛ teaspoon salt, or to taste	
2 cups plus 1 tablespoon vegetable oil, preferably canola	

In a large workbowl, whip the egg yolks, flour, Sauternes, salt, and 1 tablespoon vegetable oil with a wire whisk until a smooth batter forms. Set aside for 1 hour.

When the hour is up, in the bowl of an electric mixer set at high speed, whip the egg whites until stiff peaks form. Gently fold the egg whites into the batter.

Preheat the oven to 225°F.

In an electric fry pan or medium saucepan set over moderately high heat, heat the oil to rippling.

Dip the flowers in the batter and fry a few at a time until golden. Remove with a slotted spoon to a baking sheet lined with a double layer of paper towels to drain and place in the warm oven while you fry the remaining flowers.

In a small bowl, mix the cocoa and sugar. Dust the fried squash flowers with this mixture, place the uncooked flowers, if you have them, in the center of a serving platter, and arrange the "tempura" around them. Serve immediately.

PUFFED PUMPKIN CREPES WITH CINNAMON SUGAR AND SOUR CREAM

Makes 18 to 24 6-inch crepes serving 6 to 12

*W*e may be rule breakers, but when we make crepes we only cook them on one side. Our crepes are so thin and tender that there is no necessity, it seems to us, to flip them over. They are done when the tops have turned evenly matte with not a hint of shine and the bottoms are golden. If the crepes are to be filled and sautéed, we place the filling on the browned side and roll them up with the uncooked side on the outside, so it becomes browned in the skillet. If the crepes are to be folded or rolled and sauced, or if they are to be baked in the oven just to heat them through, we ordinarily, for aesthetic reasons, keep the browned side on the outside. Whether or not you agree with this method, these pumpkin crepes will be especially light, elegant, and delicious.

CREPES

2 cups all-purpose flour

½ teaspoon salt

4 large eggs, at room temperature

1 cup cold milk

1 cup cold water

4 tablespoons unsalted butter or margarine, melted, plus butter for the crepe pan

FILLING

½ pound farmer's cheese

2 cups canned pumpkin puree

½ cup firmly packed dark brown sugar

1 teaspoon allspice

1 teaspoon powdered ginger

2 large eggs, beaten lightly

½ cup orange marmalade

2 tablespoons unsalted butter for sautéing the filled crepes

Cinnamon sugar for sprinkling (1 teaspoon ground cinnamon mixed with 1 cup granulated sugar)

Sour cream as an accompaniment

To make the crepes, sift together the flour and the salt. Place the flour mixture and the remaining crepe ingredients in a blender or food processor and process for 1 minute. Scrape down the sides with a rubber spatula and process 20 seconds more. Place the batter in a covered jar or 4-cup measuring pitcher covered with plastic wrap and refrigerate for 2 hours or longer.

Heat a 6-inch crepe pan over moderately high heat and brush the bottom lightly with butter for the first crepe only (this one may stick, but by the second crepe the pan will be seasoned). Have the batter ready in a pitcher or the 4-cup measuring pitcher and pour about 3 tablespoons batter into the pan, tilting the pan to cover the bottom surface completely. Quickly pour any excess batter back into the pitcher, set the pan back on the heat, and cook until the surface of the crepe becomes dull and loses all its gloss. Cook a few seconds longer until the edges of the crepe pull away from the pan. Invert the pan and bang the edge sharply to release the crepe upside down onto a clean kitchen towel spread out on a work surface. Repeat the process until all the batter is used. As the crepes cool they may be stacked. (There will be a lip on each crepe where the batter was poured off. This may be trimmed with a scissors or simply tucked in when the crepes are rolled.)

To make the filling, in a large bowl, whisk together the cheese, pumpkin puree, sugar, allspice, ginger, eggs, and orange marmalade until just combined.

Place 2 heaping tablespoons of the pumpkin filling in a row slightly below the center of the browned side of the crepe. Fold the short end over the filling, then fold both sides in toward the center and roll up so that the filling is completely enclosed.

Preheat the oven to 250°F.

Heat the butter in a large skillet over moderate heat until the foam subsides. Add as many filled crepes as will fit loosely, seam side down, and sauté, turning once, until both sides are golden, about 5 minutes. Repeat with the rest of the filled crepes, keeping the sautéed ones warm in the oven until all are cooked.

Serve the crepes, 2 or 3 on a dessert plate, sprinkled with cinnamon sugar. Pass a bowl of sour cream.

Note ■ Two cups of pureed cooked carrots can be substituted for the pumpkin.

To make crepes ahead or to store excess crepes, stack the cooked and cooled crepes between sheets of wax paper, then wrap the stack in foil and freeze in batches. Well wrapped, they can keep frozen for 2 or 3 months. To thaw stacked frozen crepes, place in the refrigerator overnight. Single frozen crepes, removed from the stack, can be thawed in about ½ hour at room temperature.

CHOCOLATE-STUFFED POTATO DUMPLINGS
WITH BRANDIED APRICOT SYRUP

Serves 4 to 6

*t*his dessert is based loosely on an old Hungarian peasant recipe that was often served as a side dish, a main course, or the entire meal. The original lacked the chocolate, the ground walnuts (bread crumbs were used instead), and the brandied sauce. But our additions are merely icing on the cake, to use a dessert metaphor that, while clichéd, is nonetheless apt. Hungarian peasants, like every other Hungarian we've ever known, like their food and make the most of even the most humble ingredients. We wouldn't call this dessert humble, however.

1½ cups unseasoned mashed potatoes
   or the yield from 4 medium boiled
   potatoes mashed while still hot
6 tablespoons (¾ stick) unsalted
   butter or margarine, softened
2 heaping tablespoons all-purpose
   flour

2 large eggs, at room temperature
⅛ teaspoon salt, or to taste
1 cup semisweet chocolate bits
1 cup finely chopped walnuts
½ cup apricot jam
3 tablespoons brandy

In a large saucepan over high heat, bring 4 quarts of water to a rolling boil.

Meanwhile, in a mixing bowl, combine the mashed potatoes, 2 tablespoons butter, the flour, eggs, and salt and beat until they form a thick, unlumpy batter. Turn the batter onto a floured work surface and knead well into a smooth dough. With a large spoon, cut off enough dough to form a golf ball–sized dumpling. Press 3 or 4 chocolate bits into the center of the piece of dough, flour your hands, and roll the dough between them, making certain that the chocolate is well enclosed in the dough. Repeat with the remaining dough.

Drop the dumplings into the boiling water and cook for about 5 minutes. Taste a tiny piece of dumpling to see if it is done and transfer the dumplings with a slotted spoon to a colander or paper towels to drain.

While the dumplings are cooking, melt the remaining 4 tablespoons butter in a large skillet or sauté pan over moderately low heat. Add the chopped walnuts and brown them lightly, stirring occasionally. Transfer the drained dumplings to the skillet and roll them in the nuts with a wooden spoon until they are well coated. Transfer the dumplings to a warm serving dish, spooning any walnuts remaining in the pan over them, and keep warm while you make the sauce (or make the sauce ahead of time and keep it warm over very low heat).

In a small saucepan over moderate heat, melt the apricot jam with the brandy, stirring until it becomes syrupy. (Add a little hot water or more brandy if it remains thick.) Pour into a gravy boat or small bowl and bring to the table along with the dumplings.

Depending on their size, place 2 or 3 dumplings on each plate, spoon over a little of the syrup, and serve immediately so that the melted chocolate centers ooze out when a dumpling is cut with a fork or spoon.

Note ■ This is a substantial dessert as it stands, but a dollop of whipped cream or a small scoop of vanilla ice cream sitting alongside the dumplings would not be remiss. Even lilies can be improved with a little gilding.

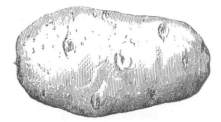

PLUM-STUFFED MASHED POTATO DUMPLINGS
IN CINNAMON TOAST CRUMBS

Serves 4 to 6

Several friends of Hungarian descent spoke rapturously about the potato-plum dessert their Hungarian-born mothers made when they were kids. None of them preserved the recipe nor could they reproduce it or describe exactly what it was that made it so special. Finally we met a Hungarian, a comparatively recent arrival here, who knew the dessert, could describe how it was made (sort of), and exactly what the ingredients were, but not their proportions. We tested and tasted and served our version to our new friend—and the old ones—and the result, set down here, brought them all back instantly to their mothers' kitchens.

1½ pounds small new potatoes	3 tablespoons granulated sugar
1 large egg, at room temperature	1 teaspoon cinnamon
½ teaspoon salt, or to taste	½ cup unseasoned, fresh white bread
5 tablespoons unsalted butter, softened	crumbs
1½ cups all-purpose flour	¼ cup sugar mixed with ¼ teaspoon cinnamon
16 ripe Italian plums, pitted but left whole	1 tablespoon finely chopped walnuts

In a medium saucepan, bring the potatoes in their skins to a boil over moderately high heat. Reduce the heat to a simmer and cook the potatoes until they are fork tender, about 15 to 20 minutes. Peel the potatoes and force them through a ricer or a food mill into a mixing bowl. Let cool.

When the potatoes are lukewarm, mix in the egg, salt, and 1 tablespoon butter with a wooden spoon. Add the flour and combine well. Knead the dough on a floured surface until the dough becomes elastic and stretch it with your fingers and the heel of your hand into a rectangle ½ inch thick. Cut the dough into 16 squares.

In the cavity left in the plums by the removal of the pits, place ½ teaspoon sugar and a pinch of cinnamon. Center a whole plum on each of the squares of dough and pull the corners together, squeezing to make a little dumpling package. If the dough should tear or is not closed completely, pinch it together so that there is no opening anywhere.

Over moderately high heat, bring a medium saucepan three-quarters full of water to a boil. Carefully drop in the dumplings and stir occasionally to prevent them from sticking to the bottom. When the dumplings rise to the surface, cook them for another 5 minutes. Remove them with a slotted spoon and set aside on paper towels to dry.

In a skillet over moderate heat, melt the remaining butter and brown the bread crumbs. Remove the breadcrumbs from the heat and mix in the cinnamon sugar. In the skillet or on a flat dish, roll the dumplings in the bread crumbs until they are coated all over. Serve immediately on warm dessert plates, 3 or 4 to a serving. Sprinkle each serving with a little of the chopped walnuts.

Note ■ Additional cinnamon sugar could be passed at the table along with additional chopped walnuts.

Alternately, the dumplings can be made ahead, then, just before serving, dipped in an egg lightly beaten with a little water, then rolled in the bread crumbs and fried in deep fat until just heated through.

The dumplings can also be made with halved fresh apricots or ½ cup apricot or plum jam substituted for the plums.

ROSEMARY-SCENTED
SWEET ITALIAN FLAT BREAD

Serves 8

Serve this aromatic sweet bread with morning coffee or afternoon tea just as you would Danish pastry. In Tuscany, where this recipe originated, it is called *schiacciata.*

½ cup warm water

½ cup plus 1 tablespoon granulated
    sugar

1½ tablespoons (1½ packages) active
    dry yeast

3 cups all-purpose flour

¾ cup raisins (preferably golden)

1 large egg, beaten

3 tablespoons fresh rosemary leaves

3 tablespoons light Tuscan olive oil

1 tablespoon vegetable shortening

Pinch of salt

In the workbowl of a food processor, combine the water with 1 tablespoon sugar. Sprinkle the yeast over the mixture and let stand for 10 minutes, or until the yeast foams.

Sprinkle 1 cup flour over the yeast mixture and process for 5 seconds. Scrape down the sides and process for 20 seconds more, or until smooth and thoroughly combined. Leave the top of the processor on and let the batter sit until doubled in volume, 30 minutes to 1½ hours.

Meanwhile, soak the raisins in warm water to cover for 20 minutes, drain, pat dry, and set aside.

When the dough has risen, add the egg, raisins, ½ cup sugar, 1 teaspoon rosemary, 1 tablespoon olive oil, the vegetable shortening, and salt. Process for 20 seconds, or until the batter is smooth. Add the remaining flour to the batter and process for 20 seconds more, or until a soft, sticky dough ball starts to form and pull away from the sides of the bowl. Turn the dough onto a floured work surface and knead it for 10 minutes, or until it is smooth and elastic.

Oil a jelly roll pan approximately 10 × 15 inches and set aside. Roll out the dough with a heavy rolling pin until it is roughly the size of the pan. Transfer the dough to the pan and with your fingers, spread it until it fits the pan. Sprinkle the top of the *schiacciata* evenly with the remaining rosemary and olive oil, cover with a dish towel, and place in a warm spot for 1½ hours, until it has risen.

Twenty minutes before you wish to bake the *schiacciata,* preheat the oven to 375°F.

Bake the *schiacciata* in the center of the oven for 20 minutes, or until the crust is golden. Serve warm or at room temperature.

Note ■ Some cooks like to sprinkle the top of the *schiacciata* with a tablespoon or two of sugar along with the rosemary and olive oil. If you like an even sweeter flat bread, by all means follow their lead. This bread is also delicious made with chopped fresh basil (in double the amount of rosemary).

CORN KERNEL SHORTCAKES WITH BERRIES 'N CREAM

Makes six 3-inch shortcakes

*t*his recipe was developed to use up one lonely uneaten ear of cooked corn. We couldn't throw it out (we never throw anything out). So we scraped off the kernels, tossed them into the food processor with some cream and vanilla, mixed them into some flour, sugar, and butter, and came up with this variation on a time-honored dish. The shortcakes are light, tender, and crumbly and flecked with yellow corn kernels to liven them up visually. They are a snap to prepare—perfect hot, warm, or at room temperature. We often serve them after a light lunch or supper, especially in the warm weather when we don't want the oven on too long—they take only 20 minutes to mix, shape, and bake.

½ cup cooked corn kernels or drained canned corn niblets

¼ cup heavy (whipping) cream

1 teaspoon pure vanilla extract

1 cup all-purpose flour

2 tablespoons granulated sugar

1 teaspoon baking powder

¼ teaspoon baking soda

½ teaspoon salt

3 tablespoons cold unsalted butter, cut into bits

Confectioners' sugar for dusting the shortcakes

Berries 'n Cream (recipe follows)

Preheat the oven to 425°F.

Lightly butter a baking sheet.

In the workbowl of a food processor, combine the corn, cream, and vanilla and pulse five or six times until the mixture is coarsely pureed. Set aside.

In a large bowl, mix together the flour, sugar, baking powder, baking soda, and salt with a fork. Add the butter to the flour mixture and blend with a pastry cutter until it resembles coarse meal. Stir in the pureed corn mixture with the fork until it forms a dough. Divide the dough in half and divide each half into three equal parts. Form each piece of dough into rough mounds on the prepared baking sheet. Bake in the center of the oven for 15 to 18 minutes, or until the shortcakes are pale golden around the edges. Transfer the shortcakes immediately to a rack to cool.

To serve, carefully cut each shortcake in half horizontally with a serrated knife and with the knife or a metal spatula, transfer each bottom half to individual dessert plates.

Top each bottom half with a portion of the Berries 'n Cream. With the knife or spatula, carefully top each serving with the top half of a shortcake. Dust with confectioners' sugar, garnish each plate with additional berries, and serve.

Note ■ Use softened fruit-flavored frozen yogurt or ice cream to fill the shortcakes instead of the flavored whipped cream. Or use plain sweetened whipped cream and garnish the shortcakes with sliced strawberries or other fruit such as peaches or apricots. We have served the shortcakes for brunch with whipped cream sweetened with a couple of tablespoons of maple syrup accompanied by sliced bananas—several breakfast food elements and flavors combined in a new way.

BERRIES 'N CREAM

1 quart ripe strawberries, raspberries, or blueberries	2 tablespoons kirsch, vodka, or framboise, or to taste
4 tablespoons granulated sugar, or to taste	1 cup well-chilled heavy (whipping) cream

Hull the strawberries. Set aside half the berries for garnish. In a bowl, mash the remaining strawberries with a fork, stir in 2 tablespoons sugar and the kirsh, and stir until the sugar is dissolved.

In a medium bowl, beat the cream with a hand mixer until it holds soft peaks. Add the remaining 2 tablespoons sugar and continue beating until it holds stiff peaks. With a rubber spatula, fold in the strawberry mixture gently but thoroughly.

APRICOT RISOTTO

Serves 8

*t*his is another of our inventions that nobody quite believes we thought of because it seems so obvious—at least to anyone who loves risotto. When we substituted fruit juice cut with water for the chicken or meat broth of the original, mascarpone, cream cheese, sour cream, or whipped cream for the Parmesan, blended chopped fresh, frozen, or canned fruit in with the cheese, and then served the risotto garnished with toasted almonds, shaved chocolate or a chocolate sauce, it became perfect brunch fare.

The secret of a creamy yet crunchy risotto is, of course, to use Italian rice (Arborio is the most widely available) and to add the hot liquid in small quantities so that the rice never "swims" in the juice mixture. The technique allows the rice to absorb the flavor of the liquid rather than merely being *boiled* in it. It should be soft on the outside and *al dente,* or resistant to the bite, on the inside and neither dry nor runny. Another secret is to never stop stirring or the rice will stick to the bottom of the pan. It takes time to get the hang of it, but even if yours doesn't come out exactly right the first time, it will still be delicious.

3 cups canned apricot nectar

2 cups water

2 tablespoons freshly squeezed lemon juice

5 tablespoons unsalted butter or margarine

2 cups Italian Arborio rice

¼ teaspoon freshly grated nutmeg

½ cup apricot brandy

1 tablespoon granulated sugar, or more to taste

¼ pound mascarpone (smooth Italian cream cheese) or whipped cream cheese, at room temperature

8 fresh halved and pitted apricots, chopped coarsely (see Note)

Optional garnishes: ½ cup finely sliced, blanched, and toasted almonds; shaved bittersweet chocolate; bittersweet chocolate sauce; or 4 additional fresh apricots, peeled, pitted, and sliced

In a medium saucepan over moderately high heat, combine the apricot nectar, water, and lemon juice and bring just to the boil; reduce the heat to a simmer.

In a heavy-bottomed saucepan or casserole, melt 3 tablespoons butter over moderate heat and when the foam subsides, add the rice and stir until it is well coated. Add the nutmeg and continue stirring for 2 minutes, then add the apricot brandy. When this is absorbed, add ½ cup simmering juice mixture and continue cooking, stirring, until the rice absorbs all the liquid. Add another ½ cup simmering juice mixture and continue to cook and stir. Continue adding liquid by the ½ cupful, decreasing the additions of liquid to ¼ cup after about 20 minutes; never let the rice "swim." When done, after about 25 to 30 minutes, the rice should be creamy, neither dry nor runny. (Caution: you may have some liquid left over; don't oversaturate the rice.) Remove the saucepan from the heat, stir in the remaining 2 tablespoons butter, and gently fold in the sugar, mascarpone, and chopped apricots until well combined.

Spoon onto individual dessert plates or into large wine glasses. Top with some of the almonds, shaved chocolate, chocolate sauce, and/or apricot slices and serve hot, warm, or at room temperature.

Note ■ Out of season use canned apricot halves, drained and chopped. Their texture is softer, but their flavor and color work well in this recipe. If you are using fresh apricots and prefer them peeled, place them in a bowl and pour boiling water over them. Let them sit for a minute and then slip off the skins.

Variations on this recipe are almost limitless. Use canned peaches, peach nectar, and peach brandy instead of apricots. Or use pear nectar and canned, fresh, or poached pears (serve this with a pitcher of hot bittersweet chocolate syrup). Scan the supermarket shelves for fruit and juice ideas and combinations. Raspberry-cranberry juice with fresh raspberries, perhaps, or with leftover cranberry sauce makes a great brunch on the Sunday after Thanksgiving. Apple juice or cider and Calvados with caramelized apple slices or warm applesauce. Orange juice with wedges of fresh, peeled oranges or orange slices. Grapefruit juice with a macedoine of fruit. The list can go on and on.

Other wines or liqueurs can be added as well. Stir about ½ cup Sauternes, brandy, port, marsala, sherry, or an appropriately flavored fruit liqueur into the sautéed rice and let it be absorbed *before* adding the first ½ cup of fruit juice mixture.

Garnishes can vary, too. Mint leaves, chopped nuts, chocolate shavings or morsels, crushed hard candies, macaroon or cookie crumbs, flavored whipped cream, ice cream, cinnamon sugar, rum-soaked raisins, and more.

Try adding a little spice along with the first addition of hot liquid: ¼ teaspoon of cinnamon or ground cloves, a dash of mace or allspice, more freshly grated nutmeg, a pinch or two of ground cardamom. You can vary the recipe according to your own taste or the juices and fruits you choose to work with.

MOCHA RISOTTO

Serves 6

*a*gain, including a rice-based dessert is stretching the vegetable theme of this book, but we don't think we'll be put in jail for it. Like corn, rice is a grain that often stands in for a vegetable, so we feel somewhat justified. Besides, this risotto is so unusual, so good, we just had to include it.

It combines two courses, dessert and coffee, and two synergistic flavors. It can be made with brewed decaffeinated to end the evening meal, if you and your guests are kept awake by regular coffee—and even with instant coffee in a pinch. Top it with whipped cream sprinkled with cinnamon sugar if you want to give it an Italian-Mexican flavor. Or stud the whipped cream topping with chocolate coffee beans or diced candied lemon peel to vary the flavors and textures. If you use some of the flavored coffee beans that have become so popular in recent years to brew your coffee, just be sure the flavoring works with the chocolate as well as the coffee.

5   cups weak brewed coffee (or alternately, 3 cups strong brewed coffee or espresso diluted with 2 cups water)

5   tablespoons unsalted butter or margarine

2   cups Italian Arborio rice (available at Italian food stores and at many specialty food stores and supermarkets)

½   cup coffee or chocolate liqueur

2   ounces (2 squares) unsweetened chocolate, chopped

4   tablespoons sugar, or to taste

¼   pound mascarpone (smooth Italian cream cheese) or whipped cream cheese

1   cup heavy (whipping) cream

1   teaspoon pure vanilla extract

Optional garnishes: ½ cup chocolate coffee beans, crushed chocolate wafers, diced candied lemon peel, or 3 tablespoons cinnamon sugar

Keep the coffee hot in a coffee maker or in a medium saucepan over moderately low heat.

In a heavy-bottomed saucepan or casserole, melt 3 tablespoons butter over moderate heat, and when the foam subsides, add the rice and stir until it is well coated. Add the liqueur, stirring, and when this is absorbed, add ½ cup hot coffee and continue to cook, stirring, until the rice absorbs all the liquid. Add another ½ cup hot coffee and continue to cook and stir. Continue adding liquid by the ½ cupful, decreasing the additions of liquid to ¼ cup after about 20 minutes; never let the rice "swim." When almost done, add the unsweetened chocolate, stirring until melted and combined. Stir in the sugar. Add more hot coffee by the tablespoonful if the mixture is too dry. When done, after about 25 to 30 minutes, the rice should be creamy, neither dry nor runny. (Caution: you may have some coffee left over; don't oversaturate the risotto.) Taste when you think the risotto is done (each grain should be tender but hold its shape and be firm, almost crunchy, on the inside). Remove the saucepan from the heat, stir in the remaining 2 tablespoons butter, and gently fold in the mascarpone until well combined.

In the large bowl of an electric mixer set on high speed, whip the cream until soft peaks form. Add the vanilla and continue to mix just until blended. Spoon the risotto into individual dessert bowls or coffee cups and serve hot, warm, or at room temperature topped with the whipped cream and the garnish of your choice.

Note ■ Our cousin, Sylvia O'Brien, a beautiful actress from Ireland and an accomplished cook, would undoubtedly transform this recipe into a meal-finale dearer to her heart, Irish Coffee Risotto. She'd simply substitute Irish whiskey for the liqueur, omit the chopped chocolate, and lace the whipped cream with more Irish whiskey.

MONT BLANC, OR POIS CHICHES GLACÉS
SNOW-CAPPED MOUNTAIN

Serves 6 to 8

*b*ecause chestnuts are seasonal, at their best in the fall, this dessert in its original French or Italian incarnation often ends a holiday meal. Our version, using glazed chickpeas, can be served anytime. As a matter of fact, it's wonderful in the summer when its resemblance to a snow-capped mountain is welcome and cooling. Its presentation at the table is spectacular. The chickpea and chocolate puree is pressed through a food mill right onto the serving platter, forming a miniature mountain of earthy-brown squiggles. The whipped cream topping is dolloped onto the pinnacle as though it were snow.

1   recipe Pois Chiches Glacés (page 173), drained, syrup reserved
2   tablespoons (¼ stick) unsalted butter, softened
6   ounces best-quality bittersweet chocolate, coarsely chopped, or semisweet chocolate bits

1   teaspoon cocoa powder
½   pint heavy (whipping) cream
1   tablespoon confectioners' sugar

In a food processor or a food mill, puree the Pois Chiches Glacés.

In a small heavy saucepan, warm ¼ cup reserved syrup over low heat. Add the butter and chocolate and stir until the chocolate is melted and incorporated into the syrup. Pour the chocolate mixture into the food processor with the pureed Pois Chiches Glacés and pulse a few times until well combined.

Using a food mill fitted with a large-holed disk, press the pureed Pois Chiches Glacés mixture directly onto a round serving platter, starting around the edge and close to the platter and working in a clockwise direction, letting the strands fall naturally. As they continue to pile up, lift the food mill and slowly spiral upward toward the center of the platter until you finish with a cone-shaped mound. Do not press or shape it. Sprinkle the mound lightly all over with the cocoa powder, using more, if necessary. Chill for at least 2 hours.

In the bowl of an electric mixer set on medium speed, whip the cream with the confectioners' sugar until it forms semistiff peaks. Using a spatula or large spoon, cover the top of the mound two-thirds of the way down with enough of the whipped cream to give the appearance of a deeply snow-covered mountain. The "snow" should not be smooth. Let it drift, with dips and peaks the way it would in nature. Serve any remaining whipped cream at the table for anyone who likes an avalanche of "snow" on his portion.

JICAMA HONEY FOOL SPIKED WITH SAGE

Serves 6

a "fool" is a dessert that usually consists of sweetened pureed stewed fruit folded into whipped cream. It's a simple, old-fashioned concoction much favored in the British Isles and it was often served at American colonists' tables. We've updated our version by using jicama, raw not stewed, flavored with an unusual combination of sage-steeped honey. You can also use basil or rosemary and substitute Bosc pears for the jicama if it is unavailable in your area. The proportions remain the same.

¼ cup honey

1 tablespoon minced fresh sage leaves

1 medium jicama (about 1 pound),
    peeled and coarsely chopped

¾ cup well-chilled heavy (whipping)
    cream

Raspberries or strawberries for
    garnish (optional)

In a small saucepan, combine the honey and the minced sage and cook, uncovered, over moderately low heat for 5 minutes. Transfer the mixture to a bowl and cover or leave in the pan, covered, overnight.

In a food processor, pulse the jicama, stopping and scraping down the sides several times, until it is a smooth puree. Reheat the honey mixture, pour into the processor, and blend with the jicama. Pour into a bowl and chill the mixture for 1 to 2 hours, or until very cold.

In the chilled bowl of an electric mixer or with a hand mixer set on moderately high speed, whip the cream until it holds stiff peaks. With a spatula, fold the whipped cream gently but thoroughly into the jicama-honey mixture. Pour into 6 dessert glasses or bowls and chill, covered, for 3 hours. Decorate with 2 or 3 fresh raspberries or a strawberry, if desired.

ICE CREAMS AND FROZEN DESSERTS

Let your freezer or ice cream maker do the work. These frozen delights can be stirred up in minutes by hand or in a food processor. Then you just allow electricity and temperature to take over. All very uncomplicated but the final result is elegant and sophisticated.

The easiest of all is probably the Granita di Basilico, basil ice. Its fresh-from-the-garden flavor is a revelation—sweet, summery, cool—completely unexpected.

The transformation of basil from an herb familiar mostly from pesto and tomato dishes into a seductive frozen dessert is typical of the versatility and endless possibilities of vegetables in sweet concoctions.

Basil and Fresh Peach Ice Cream ■ Semifreddo ai Pois Chiches

Glacés, or Frozen Cream Dessert with Mock Glacéed Chestnuts ■

Granita di Basilico, or Basil Semisoft Ice ■ Granita di Finocchio

con Crema di Caffè, or Fennel Ice with Coffee Cream ■

Ginger Frozen Yogurt ■ Molded Cold Pumpkin Soufflé Lined with

Grand Marnier–Soaked Ladyfingers ■ Rosy Red Bean Ice Cream

with Raspberry Sauce ■ Sweet Potato Banana Chip Ice Cream

BASIL AND FRESH PEACH ICE CREAM

Makes 1 quart

*b*asil grows in such profusion in Italy that its flavor and aroma seems to perfume the air in the countryside—even the grapes and peaches. Consequently, eating Italian peaches is an experience unlike eating even the best the United States has to offer, and they inspired this ice cream recipe. Using fresh basil essence to intensify the peach-basil marriage is the kind of underscoring that we find works spectacularly in a frozen dessert such as this. It nourishes rather than destroys the seductive peach flavor, making us reel with memories of wiping peach juice from our chins while breathing the basil-scented air of Anacapri or Ansedonia.

1½ pounds of ripe peaches (about 3 large), washed and patted dry	½ cup heavy (whipping) cream
½ cup firmly packed light brown sugar, or more to taste	⅓ cup finely chopped fresh basil leaves
1 tablespoon fresh lime juice	¼ teaspoon finely grated lime zest
1 cup half-and-half or Homemade Crème Fraîche (page 100)	Pinch of salt
	Basil flowers or peach slices for garnish

Place the peaches in a large heatproof bowl and pour boiling water over them. Let them steep for 30 seconds to 1 minute, pour off the water, and when the peaches are cool enough to handle, peel off the skins and discard. Cut the peaches in half and discard the pits. Cut the peach halves into coarse chunks. Put the peach chunks, sugar, and lime juice into the workbowl of a food processor and pulse a few times to a thick, chunky consistency; do not puree. Set aside.

Into a medium saucepan set over moderately high heat, pour the half-and-half and heavy cream; add the basil leaves, lime zest, and salt and scald the cream mixture for 4 to 5 minutes, never letting it boil. Set the saucepan in a larger bowl of ice water and cool to room temperature. Chill in the refrigerator for at least 1 hour. When very cold, strain the cream mixture through a fine metal sieve into the peach mixture, pressing down on the solids to extract as much basil essence as possible. (If a few tiny bits of basil leaf find their way into the mixture, so much the better.) Stir well and freeze in an ice cream maker according to the manufacturer's instructions.

SEMIFREDDO AI POIS CHICHES GLACÉS, OR FROZEN CREAM DESSERT WITH MOCK GLACÉED CHESTNUTS

Serves 8 to 10

*W*e are Italophiles. So, although this is not a real Italian dessert, it is Italian in concept, style, and spirit. And who is to say that an Italian cook somewhere hasn't thought of this using real marrons glacés, which are easy to come by in Italy, where chestnut trees abound.

½ cup currants

⅓ cup dark rum

4 large eggs, separated

⅓ cup granulated sugar

1 recipe Pois Chiches Glacés (page 173), drained (syrup reserved), and pureed

2 cups heavy (whipping) cream

1 cup coarsely crushed Italian macaroons (Amaretti di Saronno)

2 tablespoons grated semisweet chocolate for garnish

Oil a 2-quart loaf pan or charlotte mold.

Macerate the currants in the rum for 1 hour or more.

With an electric mixer set on high speed, beat the egg yolks for 30 seconds. Continue beating, adding the sugar gradually, until the mixture becomes thick and lemon colored. On medium speed, add the pureed Pois Chiches Glacés, the currants, and the rum and beat until well combined.

Whip the cream until stiff peaks form. With clean beaters, whip the egg whites in a separate bowl until stiff peaks form. With a rubber spatula, fold the whipped cream into the pureed mixture, then fold in the beaten egg whites and the crushed macaroons.

Pour the mixture into the prepared mold. Cover tightly with plastic wrap, then foil. Place in the freezer for at least 6 hours or up to a week.

To unmold, remove the wrappings and center the inverted mold onto a serving platter. Hold a hair dryer set on high several inches from the mold and move it back and forth around the mold for a few seconds. Lift off the mold. Drizzle the reserved syrup over the top and sprinkle with the grated chocolate. Serve immediately in thick slices with some of the syrup.

GRANITA DI BASILICO, OR BASIL SEMISOFT ICE

Serves 4 to 6

*t*his is a cooling way to finish a summer meal. Granite, the semisoft ices of Italy, are the way Italians refresh themselves on a hot afternoon. Our granita is flavored with a fresh basil syrup and, if the Italians ever discover it, could replace the perennial favorite, *granita di caffè*, in popularity. We suggest it as a dessert, alone, with Raspberry Sauce (page 168), or strewn with berries or slices of fresh fruit, or perhaps with a splash of crème de menthe. But it could also be served as an *entremet* during a very formal meal to refresh the palate between courses. Two tablespoons (or more to taste) of fresh thyme, sage, or marjoram can also be turned into refreshing granite. But we still like basil best.

3 cups water

1 cup granulated sugar

1 cup chopped fresh basil leaves

2 tablespoons lemon juice

In a small saucepan over high heat, combine the water and sugar and bring to a boil. Reduce the heat and simmer for 3 minutes. Add basil and stir. Cover tightly and set aside for 15 minutes.

Meanwhile, line a sieve with cheesecloth and place the sieve over a bowl. When the basil mixture is ready, strain it, extracting as much liquid as possible by pressing the solids with the back of a wooden spoon. Discard the basil leaves. Add the lemon juice to the liquid, stir well, and pour into a shallow pan, an 8-inch loaf pan, or an ice cube tray. Place in the freezer until almost firm, about 2 hours, stirring every 20 to 30 minutes to break up the ice crystals, especially those at the sides of the container where the granita tends to freeze first and can become solid. If the granita becomes too solid, scrape away at the surface with a wooden spoon until it is all a mass of tiny ice crystals. Alternately, pour the chilled mixture into an ice cream machine and freeze according to the manu-facturer's instructions.

Serve in glass goblets or champagne glasses topped with berries, sliced fresh fruit, or Raspberry Sauce.

GRANITA DI FINOCCHIO CON CREMA DI CAFFÈ, OR FENNEL ICE WITH COFFEE CREAM

Serves 6 to 8

*i*talians really know their ices—and ice creams. We've adapted the Italian method for this unusual ice using a favorite ingredient, fennel. The subtle licorice flavor is refreshing, especially under the luxurious coffee cream topping.

1½ cups granulated sugar

2 cups water

4 cups (about 1½ pounds) trimmed and coarsely chopped fennel bulbs plus 2 tablespoons chopped green feathery fronds

1 tablespoon Sambuca or other anise-flavored liqueur

1 recipe Coffee Cream (recipe follows) Cinnamon for dusting

In a medium saucepan over moderately high heat, combine the sugar, water, and chopped fennel and bring to a boil. Reduce the heat to a simmer and cook for 20 minutes, or until the fennel is very tender. Remove from the heat and let cool.

Puree the cooled fennel mixture with its liquid in a food processor, blender, or food mill. Add the chopped fennel fronds and the Sambuca, pour the mixture into a shallow pan, 8-inch loaf pan, or ice cube trays and freeze for 2 to 3 hours, or until the mixture begins to harden. Remove from the freezer and beat with an electric mixer or process in a food processor until smooth and creamy. Return to the freezer and freeze solid. Thirty minutes to 1 hour before serving, remove from the freezer and place in the refrigerator to let the ice soften to eating consistency.

Alternately, pour mixture into an ice cream machine and freeze according to the manufacturer's instructions.

Serve in large wine glasses, goblets, or glass dessert bowls topped with the Coffee Cream dusted with cinnamon.

CREMA DI CAFFÈ, or COFFEE CREAM

1 cup heavy (whipping) cream

¼ cup strong brewed espresso or 1
    teaspoon instant espresso powder
    dissolved in ¼ cup boiling water,
    cooled

¼ cup confectioners' sugar

In an electric mixer set on medium speed, whip the cream until soft peaks form. In a small bowl, mix the espresso with the sugar and stir just to combine. Whip the cream again, adding the espresso mixture little by little until well combined. The cream should be fluffy yet smooth, not stiff.

GINGER FROZEN YOGURT

Makes 1½ quarts

a lot less caloric (especially if you use low-fat or no-fat plain yogurt) and so easy to make, this frozen dessert gets its flavor from both fresh and crystallized ginger. The only effort on your part is finely chopping the crystallized ginger and peeling and grating the fresh ginger. This can be turned into a mango-ginger frozen yogurt by reducing the amount of yogurt to 2½ pints and adding to the mixture a 1-pound fresh mango, peeled, all the flesh cut from the pit and chopped fine by hand or pureed in the processor.

1½ teaspoons grated peeled fresh
    gingerroot

¾ cup finely chopped crystallized
    ginger

3 pints plain yogurt (regular, low-fat,
    or no-fat)

½ teaspoon pure vanilla extract

2 tablespoons granulated sugar, or
    more to taste

In a large bowl, stir together the fresh gingerroot and crystallized ginger with the yogurt, vanilla, and sugar until well combined. Taste and add more sugar if you like. Freeze the mixture in an ice cream maker according to the manufacturer's instructions.

MOLDED COLD PUMPKIN SOUFFLÉ LINED WITH GRAND MARNIER–SOAKED LADYFINGERS

Serves 6

*d*on't wait for Thanksgiving to serve this dessert. It's delicious anytime—especially during warmer weather. It's a cold, spicy grand finale that's a nice change from ice cream, is spectacular looking, and so easy to make with canned unseasoned pumpkin puree. We serve it au naturel or drizzled with a caramel or Grand Marnier sauce at the table. But lightly whipped cream or a bittersweet chocolate sauce would be just as festive. If you own a footed cake stand (we collect them), serve it on that and make it look really fancy by piping a border of whipped cream rosettes all around the bottom edge, each one topped with a ¼-inch piece of crystallized ginger.

2 tablespoons Grand Marnier	1 cup firmly packed light brown sugar
12 or 14 good-quality dry, tender (not spongy) ladyfingers	½ teaspoon allspice
	½ teaspoon freshly grated nutmeg
2 tablespoons (2 envelopes) unflavored gelatin	1 teaspoon cinnamon
	1 teaspoon powdered ginger
¼ cup cold water	6 large eggs, separated, at room temperature
2 cups canned or homemade pumpkin puree	1 cup heavy (whipping) cream

Butter an 8-cup charlotte mold, soufflé dish, or other cylindrical mold 3½ to 4 inches deep.

In a shallow soup plate, dilute the Grand Marnier with 1 tablespoon water. Dip the flat side of each ladyfinger in the Grand Marnier mixture and place upright, pressed closely together with their curved sides against the buttered sides of the mold. (Even if your mold is slanted outward, the Grand Marnier softens the ladyfingers sufficiently to make them fit snugly at their bottom ends.) Set aside.

Sprinkle the gelatin over the cold water and let stand to soften, about 5 minutes.

In a small saucepan over moderate heat, combine the pumpkin puree, brown sugar, allspice, nutmeg, cinnamon, and ginger and bring to a boil, stirring, until the sugar is dissolved. Remove from the heat.

Beat the egg yolks and whisk them into the pumpkin mixture briskly until well combined and smooth. Return to the heat and cook for 2 to 3 minutes, stirring constantly. Remove from the heat and whisk in the softened gelatin, whisking until it is dissolved. Pour and scrape the mixture into a large bowl and set aside to cool until just barely warm, stirring occasionally.

With an electric mixer set on high speed, beat the egg whites until they hold stiff peaks and with a rubber spatula, fold them into the pumpkin mixture until thoroughly blended. With an electric mixer set on moderately high speed and using clean blades, beat the whipped cream until it holds stiff peaks and fold it into the pumpkin mixture. Pour into the ladyfinger-lined mold, smoothing the top with a metal spatula. Chill for 2 hours or up to 24 hours. Run a thin sharp knife around the edge of the mold to release. Place a serving dish over the mold and invert both. Remove the mold. If the mold does not slip off easily, hold a hair dryer set on its lowest setting at least 8 inches from the mold and quickly blow hot air over the bottom and sides. The mold should slip off with no problem. Cut the soufflé in wedges 2 ladyfingers wide.

ROSY RED BEAN ICE CREAM WITH RASPBERRY SAUCE

Serves 6 to 8

*R*ed bean ice cream is an Asian invention. We add more beans and whipped cream, and spoon raspberry sauce over each portion for good measure.

1½ cups confectioners' sugar, sifted

6 large egg yolks

2 cups milk, scalded and kept hot

2 cups heavy (whipping) cream, chilled

2 cups adzuki bean puree made from unseasoned home-cooked beans

Raspberry Sauce (recipe follows)

In the bowl of an electric mixer set on medium speed, beat the sugar with the egg yolks until light and lemon colored. Reduce the speed to low and add the hot scalded milk in a stream, beating until well combined. Transfer the custard to a heavy medium saucepan and cook over moderate heat, stirring with a wooden spoon, until thickened enough to coat the back of the spoon, about 5 to 7 minutes. Strain the mixture through a fine sieve into a metal bowl set in a bowl of ice and let cool, stirring occasionally, for 1 hour.

In a well-chilled bowl, beat the cream until it forms soft peaks. With a rubber spatula, fold one-third of the cream into the bean puree to lighten it, then gently but thoroughly fold in the remaining cream. Fold the chilled custard into the bean mixture until well combined. Freeze in an ice cream freezer according to the manufacturer's instructions. Serve with Raspberry Sauce.

RASPBERRY SAUCE

1 10-ounce package frozen raspberries in syrup, thawed

2 tablespoons granulated sugar

1 tablespoon framboise (raspberry liqueur), kirsch, or brandy

In a blender or food processor, puree the raspberries, sugar, and framboise. Strain the puree through a fine metal sieve into a bowl, pressing down hard on the solids. Serve chilled or at room temperature.

SWEET POTATO BANANA CHIP ICE CREAM

Makes about 1½ pints

*R*emember those Thanksgiving casseroles of searingly hot mashed sweet potatoes mixed with canned pineapple chunks, then topped with brown sugar and marshmallows? Just seeing that quartet in print gives us a toothache. Sweet upon sweet upon sweet. Whoever thought that one up? And why did it become so popular? The sweet potato and pineapple combo isn't too bad, but we think sweet potatoes and banana chips are much better. Banana chips—look for them in cellophane bags at your supermarket or health food store—are wonderfully crunchy and add a surprising, welcome texture to this mildly spiced, earthy-tasting, and not-too-sweet ice cream.

1 cup milk	½ teaspoon ground cloves
4 large egg yolks	1 cup sweet potato puree (made from
⅔ cup firmly packed light or dark	drained and rinsed canned "yams"
brown sugar	or home-baked sweet potatoes)
⅛ teaspoon salt	1 cup heavy (whipping) cream
1 teaspoon cinnamon	¼ teaspoon pure vanilla extract (or 1
½ teaspoon powdered ginger	teaspoon bourbon)
1 teaspoon freshly ground nutmeg	1 cup lightly crushed banana chips

In a small saucepan, scald the milk and keep warm over the lowest possible heat.

In a large bowl, beat the egg yolks with a wire whisk until light and frothy. Whisk in the sugar, salt, cinnamon, ginger, nutmeg, and cloves until well blended. Add the hot milk in a slow stream, whisking constantly. Pour the egg mixture into the top of a double boiler over barely simmering water and cook, stirring constantly, 5 to 8 minutes, or until the mixture coats the back of a spoon. Remove from the heat and whisk in the sweet potato puree. Cool to room temperature and whisk in the cream and vanilla until thoroughly blended. Fold in the banana chips and chill in the refrigerator for at least 1 hour. Freeze in an ice cream maker according to the manufacturer's instructions.

Note ■ If calories are no problem, serve this ice cream as a sundae topped with bittersweet chocolate sauce and crushed gingersnaps. Or, if you really miss those treacly Thanksgiving casseroles, serve with Marshmallow Fluff and crushed pineapple.

CONFECTIONS, JAMS, AND PRESERVES

These are sweets to serve after you've served the sweets, or anytime your craving for sugary tastes takes over. If you like truffles, try our version made with faux marrons glacés, chickpeas disguised as glazed chestnuts (a recipe that is the basis for many deceptively rich, yet oddly nutritious desserts in this book). Halwa lovers have a new taste sensation in store when they bite into Carrot Halwa with Raisins and Pistachios. All these "candies" reward you with lots of adventurous flavor but very little investment in effort.

In this chapter, we also introduce you to our new vegetable spreads. They are wonderful on breakfast toast, on muffins, or in tea sandwiches. They can also be spooned over ice creams or puddings to flavor them. They make great fillings for tarts, tartlets, or cookies. Their flavors don't take any getting used to. They seem natural and inevitable in spite of the fact that they are brand new.

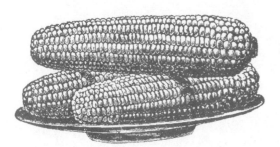

CONFECTIONS ■ *Pois Chiches Glacés (Faux Marrons Glacés, or Glazed Chickpeas)* ■ *Carrot Halwa with Raisins and Pistachios* ■ *Chocolate Pois Chiches Glacés Truffles* ■ *Chocolate Pâté*

JAMS AND PRESERVES ■ *Fresh Beet and Orange Jam* ■ *Pumpkin, Ginger, and Apricot Preserves* ■ *French Red Tomato Jam Two Ways*

POIS CHICHES GLACÉS (FAUX MARRONS GLACÉS, OR GLAZED CHICKPEAS)

Makes about 4 cups

*b*ottled or canned peeled whole chestnuts from France are available at most food specialty stores—at a price. However, when you think of how tedious roasting chestnuts, then peeling them is, the high price you pay seems almost worth it. We have devised a substitute that is so similar in taste and texture that even our friend and marrons glacés maven, Elliot Oxenberg, can't tell the difference—blindfolded. Blindfolded because chickpeas are prettier than glazed chestnuts. For one thing they are a creamy beige color rather than a brownish gray. They also look like miniature ram's heads, so they can be used whole as decoration around the edge of an iced cake or around its base. The price? About a fifth or less that of the real thing, which makes them even sweeter.

1½ cups water
1½ cups granulated sugar
½ teaspoon fresh lemon juice
1 tablespoon pure vanilla extract
1 tablespoon unsweetened cocoa
   powder

1 19-ounce can chickpeas, drained
   and rinsed
3 to 4 tablespoons dark rum or
   cognac

In a heavy medium saucepan, bring the water, sugar, lemon juice, vanilla extract, and cocoa to a boil over moderate heat, washing down any sugar crystals clinging to the sides of the pan with a brush dipped in cold water, until the sugar is dissolved. Add the chickpeas, turn the heat down to simmer, and cook, stirring occasionally, for 10 minutes.

With a slotted spoon, transfer the chickpeas to a sterilized 1-quart Mason jar or two 1-pint jars (prepared for canning according to the manufacturer's instructions, or see page 178 if you want to keep the glazed chickpeas on the shelf indefinitely) or into a container with a tight-fitting lid (if you just want to store them in the refrigerator for up to 5 weeks).

Boil the syrup remaining in the saucepan for 10 to 15 minutes, or until it thickens to the consistency of honey. Stir in the rum, pour the hot syrup over the chickpeas, and seal the jars.

CARROT HALWA WITH RAISINS AND PISTACHIOS

Serves 8

*t*his Indian sweet is often served with black coffee after a rich meal. It's not flaky and creamy like the packaged halvah we're used to—that's Middle Eastern, made with heavy cream and sesame seeds. This is almost like an orange-hued fudge flecked with green pistachios and yellow raisins. It can also be made with pumpkin puree, grated zucchini, or mashed potatoes.

3 cups peeled and finely grated carrots
   (about 1 pound, trimmed)

2 cups milk

2 tablespoons honey

½ cup granulated sugar

½ teaspoon ground cardamom

½ teaspoon cinnamon

4 tablespoons (½ stick) unsalted butter

¼ cup golden raisins

½ cup pistachios

Silver sprinkles for decorating
   (optional)

In a large, heavy-bottomed saucepan, combine the carrots and milk and bring to a boil over high heat. Reduce the heat to a simmer and cook the mixture, stirring occasionally, for 1 hour or more, until the liquid has almost been absorbed and the mixture is thick. Continue cooking, stirring constantly, until the liquid has evaporated completely. Add the honey, sugar, cardamom, cinnamon, and butter and continue cooking, stirring vigorously with a wooden spoon, until the mixture is almost dry and starts to pull away from the pan (it may take 20 minutes or more). Stir in the raisins and ¼ cup pistachios until well combined. Scrape onto a large, buttered dinner plate or serving platter and shape into a thick disk. Chop the remaining pistachios and sprinkle them over the halwa along with the silver sprinkles if used. Let cool and set, then cut diagonally into diamond shapes. Serve at room temperature or cold.

CHOCOLATE POIS CHICHES GLACÉS TRUFFLES

Makes about 2 dozen truffles

*I*f you plan ahead at holiday time, you can have quantities of candied chickpeas on hand to make delicious confections such as this one to serve to guests or to package prettily and give as gifts to very special friends and family. We suggest dividing the truffles among several decorative tins or other airtight containers and keeping the containers chilled for up to a week. Before presenting, wrap the tins in colored tissue—then caution the recipient to store in the refrigerator (if they can resist devouring them on the spot) and to finish them up before another week is out.

¼ cup heavy (whipping) cream

6 ounces best-quality bittersweet
   chocolate, finely chopped

2 tablespoons dark rum or brandy

¾ cup Pois Chiches Glacés (page 173),
   drained and finely chopped

¼ cup unsweetened cocoa powder for
   coating the truffles

In a small saucepan, bring the cream just to a boil over moderately high heat. Remove the pan from the heat and whisk in the chocolate, whisking until the chocolate is completely melted and combined with the cream. Whisk in the rum and continue to whisk until the mixture is smooth. Stir in the Pois Chiches Glacés until dispersed and chill the mixture, covered, for 3 hours, or until it is firm. Form the mixture by heaping teaspoonsful into balls and roll the balls in the cocoa powder to coat. (Handle the truffles as little as possible or body heat will melt them.) Chill the truffles on a baking sheet lined with wax paper for 1 hour, or until they are firm. Transfer to airtight containers and keep chilled for up to 2 weeks.

CHOCOLATE PÂTÉ

Serves 6 to 8

*W*e call this a pâté because it is rich, dense, and formed into a pâtélike loaf to be served in thin slices. The slices can be accompanied by whipped cream and strawberries or placed in a pool of raspberry puree. They can be doused with custard sauces or sprinkled with chopped nuts. The loaf can be presented decorated with stripes and squiggles of hazelnut butter cream, rosettes of liqueur-flavored whipped cream, or a dozen or more different garnishes. But this dessert is so rich it needs none of them.

½ cup (1 stick) unsalted butter

5 ounces best-quality bittersweet chocolate

1 recipe Pois Chiches Glacés (page 173)

2 tablespoons Frangelico (hazelnut liqueur)

1 cup confectioners' sugar

1 tablespoon cocoa powder

½ teaspoon pure vanilla extract

In a small skillet over moderately high heat, melt the butter and when the foam subsides cook it for 1 or 2 minutes, watching carefully, until it turns a nut brown (do not burn). Remove the skillet from the heat and add the chocolate, stirring, until the chocolate melts and combines well with the butter.

Drain the Pois Chiches Glacés (reserving the syrup for another use) and puree them in a food processor along with the hazelnut liqueur until smooth. Add the chocolate mixture, the sugar, cocoa powder, and vanilla to the pureed beans and pulse several times until completely incorporated.

Brush a small loaf pan, 3- to 4-cup capacity, with flavorless salad oil. Press the chocolate-bean mixture into the mold, packing it down firmly. Smooth the top, cover with plastic wrap, and refrigerate for 4 hours or up to 24 hours.

Remove the plastic wrap, cover the pan with a small, preferably oblong, platter, and invert. Using a hair dryer set on high heat and held at least 8 inches away, make several passes over and around the mold, stopping and testing often, until the mold releases easily. Return the pâté to the refrigerator until serving time. Garnish as you wish or serve unadorned in thin slices.

FRESH BEET AND ORANGE JAM

Makes about 1 pint

*t*his deep, dark magenta–colored jam spreads joy on hot biscuits or muffins, or can fill crepes, cookies, or tarts with its fascinating combination of flavors. We know there are lots of people who dislike beets, but we defy even those dissenters to pass up this jam.

1½ pounds beets, trimmed and peeled	½ teaspoon cinnamon
1 large orange	½ teaspoon allspice
1 lemon	2 cups granulated sugar

Cut the beets into small chunks, place them in a food processor, and pulse them several times until finely grated.

Remove the zest from the orange and the lemon using a vegetable peeler or zester and finely mince. Set aside. Cut the two fruits in half and remove any pits. Into a measuring cup, squeeze the juice from the orange and lemon. Reserve the squeezed carcasses of the fruits (the intermediate white layer, or pith, contains pectin, which will help bind the jam). If necessary, add enough water to the juices to make ¾ cup liquid.

In a medium saucepan over moderately high heat, bring the juice mixture to a boil. Add the grated beets, cinnamon, allspice, and reserved fruit carcasses, cover, and cook for 10 minutes, or until the beets are tender and the mixture is somewhat dry. With tongs, pick out and discard the fruit carcasses, first scraping any beets that cling to them back into the pan. Add the reserved zests and the sugar to the beet mixture, return to a boil, and cook, stirring, until the sugar dissolves. Taste and adjust the seasonings. Lower the heat to moderate and continue to cook, uncovered, stirring often, until thick, about 25 to 30 minutes. Pour into hot, sterilized jars to within a quarter inch of the rims, seal, and process according to the manufacturer's instructions or see page 178.

Alternately, when the jam is thick, turn off the heat, cool in the pan, and spoon or pour into jars or plastic containers with tight-fitting lids and refrigerate. The jam will keep in the refrigerator for 1 month to 6 weeks.

Variation ■ For Fresh Carrot and Orange Jam, substitute an equal amount of carrots for the beets, 1 tablespoon pure vanilla extract and 1 teaspoon ground cardamom for the cinnamon and allspice, and proceed as above.

PUMPKIN, GINGER, AND APRICOT PRESERVES

Makes about 4 cups

*t*his recipe doesn't date back very far—only to the writing of this book, as a matter of fact—but it does add an old-fashioned, down-home flavor to buttered biscuits, French Toast, and as a topping for ice cream. It can also be used as a tart filling.

½ pound dried apricots

5 cups fresh peeled and seeded
    pumpkin (about 4–5 pounds
    whole), cut in ½-inch dice

1 tablespoon peeled and grated fresh
    gingerroot

1 3-inch cinnamon stick

2½ cups granulated sugar

In a bowl, let the apricots soak in 1½ cups water, covered, overnight. Drain the apricots, reserving the water, and cut them into ¼-inch julienne strips.

In a large saucepan, combine the reserved water, the pumpkin, the gingerroot, and the cinnamon stick, and bring to a boil over high heat. Turn the heat down to simmer and cook the mixture, covered, stirring occasionally, for 30 minutes. Discard the cinnamon stick.

In a food processor or blender, puree the pumpkin mixture with any of its liquid and return it to the pan over moderate heat. Add the apricots and the sugar. Bring the mixture to a boil, stirring, turn the heat down to simmer, and cook, uncovered, for 30 minutes, or until it is thickened.

Spoon the preserves into hot, sterilized Mason-type canning jars, filling the jars to within ¼ inch of the rims. Wipe the rims with a dampened cloth or paper towel and seal the jars with the sterilized lids. Place the jars in a canning kettle or a deep steamer and add enough water to cover the jars by 2 inches. Bring the water to a boil over high heat and boil the jars for 10 minutes. With tongs, transfer the jars to a dish towel to drain and cool.

Note ■ Don't throw out the pumpkin seeds. Spread them out on a cookie sheet and dry them in a 350°F. oven for about 30 minutes. They're delicious as nutritious snacks or to nibble with cocktails.

FRENCH RED TOMATO JAM TWO WAYS

Technique No. 1 makes 2–3 one-pint jars
Technique No. 2 makes 3–4 one-pint jars

*L*ots of French food—Paris-chic French food—is pretentious, overcooked, fussy, and requires techniques and ingredients not at the fingertips of most American cooks. Country French, like the rural and peasant foods of most countries, is far easier to cook—and tastier. These provincial tomato jams are simple, straightforward. They taste of tomatoes, of the sun—and take to buttered toast or muffins or to tart fillings like your favorite fruit jams. Here we propose two techniques using the same quantities: the first technique accomplishes a smooth-textured jam, the second a chunky one.

2 pounds red ripe tomatoes (regular or plum), quartered	3 cups granulated sugar
¾ pound Granny Smith or Greening apples, cored but not peeled	¼ teaspoon cinnamon
⅔ cup apple juice, cider, or water	2 whole cloves
	Juice and grated rind of 2 lemons

TECHNIQUE NO. 1

In a saucepan, cook the tomatoes and apples in the apple juice gently over moderate heat until they are tender. Do not drain. Force through a food mill to remove seeds and skins (or, if you prefer, puree in a food processor and press through a sieve). Return the puree to the pan over moderately low heat and add the sugar, cinnamon, cloves, lemon juice, and lemon rind, stirring to combine well. When the sugar has dissolved, turn the heat to high, bring to a rapid boil, and cook, stirring occasionally to prevent sticking, until thickened, about 20 to 30 minutes. Test for the setting point with a candy thermometer (it should register 220°F.), or by pouring a few drops on a chilled saucer. Let cool. It is ready if the jam wrinkles when one side is lightly pressed. If not, return to the heat and boil a few minutes more, then test again. Remove from the heat and discard the cloves. Pour into hot, sterilized jars and seal according to the manufacturer's instructions.

TECHNIQUE NO. 2

Peel and seed the tomato quarters; peel and core the apples. Cut both into ½-inch pieces. Cook in the juice until tender. Do not drain or puree. Just add the remaining ingredients and proceed as in Technique No. 1.

INDEX

CONVERSION CHART

Equivalent Imperial and Metric Measurements

American cooks use standard containers, the 8-ounce cup and a tablespoon that takes exactly 16 level fillings to fill that cup level. Measuring by cup makes it very difficult to give weight equivalents, as a cup of densely packed butter will weigh considerably more than a cup of flour. The easiest way therefore to deal with cup measurements in recipes is to take the amount by volume rather than by weight. Thus the equation reads:

1 cup = 240 ml = 8 fl.oz. 1/2 cup = 120 ml = 4 fl.oz.

It is possible to buy a set of American cup measures in major stores around the world.

In the States, butter is often measured in sticks. One stick is the equivalent of 8 tablespoons. One tablespoon of butter is therefore the equivalent to 1/2 ounce/15 grams.

Linear Measure

1 inch	2.54 centimeters
1 foot	0.3048 meters
1 yard	0.9144 meters
1 mile	1.609 meters

Area Measure

1 square inch	6.4516 square centimeters
1 square foot	929.03 square centimeters
1 square yard	0.836 square meters
1 acre	0.405 hectares
1 square mile	2.5899 square kilometers

Liquid Measures

Fluid ounces	U.S. measures	Imperial measures	Milliliters
	1 TSP	1 TSP	5
1/4	2 TSP	1 DESSERTSPOON	7
1/2	1 TBS	1 TBS	15
1	2 TBS	2 TBS	28
2	1/4 CUP	4 TBS	56
4	1/2 CUP OR 1/4 PINT		110
5		1/4 PINT OR 1 GILL	140
6	3/4 CUP		170
8	1 CUP OR 1/2 PINT		225
9			250, 1/4 LITER
10	1 1/4 CUPS	1/2 PINT	280
12	1 1/2 CUPS OR 3/4 PINT		240
15		3/4 PINT	420
16	2 CUPS OR 1 PINT		450
18	2 1/4 CUPS		500, 1/2 LITER
20	2 1/2 CUPS	1 PINT	560
24	3 CUPS OR 1 1/2 PINTS		675
25		1 1/4 PINTS	700
27	3 1/2 CUPS		750
30	3 3/4 CUPS	1 1/2 PINTS	840
32	4 CUPS OR 2 PINTS OR 1 QUART		900
35		1 3/4 PINTS	980
36	4 1/2 CUPS		1000, 1 LITER
40	5 CUPS OR 2 1/2 PINTS	2 PINTS OR 1 QUART	1120
48	6 CUPS OR 3 PINTS		1350
50		2 1/2 PINTS	1400
60	7 1/2 CUPS	3 PINTS	1680
64	8 CUPS OR 4 PINTS OR 2 QUARTS		1800
72	9 CUPS		2000, 2 LITERS
80	10 CUPS OR 5 PINTS	4 PINTS	2250
96	12 CUPS OR 3 QUARTS		2700
100		5 PINTS	2800

Solid Measures

U.S. and Imperial Measures		Metric Measures	
OUNCES	POUNDS	GRAMS	KILOS
1		28	
2		56	
3 1/2		100	
4	1/4	112	
5		140	
6		168	
8	1/2	225	
9		250	1/4
12	3/4	340	
16	1	450	
18		500	1/2
20	1 1/4	560	
24	1 1/2	675	
27		750	3/4
28	1 3/4	780	
32	2	900	
36	2 1/4	1000	1
40	2 1/2	1100	
48	3	1350	
54		1500	1 1/2
64	4	1800	
72	4 1/2	2000	2
80	5	2250	2 1/4
90		2500	2 1/2
100	6	2800	2 3/4

Suggested Equivalents and Substitutes for Ingredients

all-purpose flour—plain flour
arugula—rocket
beet—beetroot
confectioner's sugar—icing sugar
cornstarch—cornflour
eggplant—aubergine
granulated sugar—caster sugar
kielbasa—Polish sausage
lima beans—broad beans
pearl onions—pickling onions
scallion—spring onion
shortening—white fat
snow pea—mangetout
sour cherry—morello cherry
squab—poussin
squash—courgettes or marrow
unbleached flour—strong, white flour
vanilla bean—vanilla pod
zest—rind
zucchini—courgettes
light cream—single cream
heavy cream—double cream
half and half—12% fat milk
buttermilk—ordinary milk
sour milk—add 1 tablespoon vinegar or
  lemon juice to 1 cup minus 1 tablespoon
  lukewarm water. Let stand for 5 minutes.
cheesecloth—muslin

Oven Temperature Equivalents

Fahrenheit	Celsius	Gas Mark	Description
225	110	1/4	Cool
250	130	1/2	
275	140	1	Very Slow
300	150	2	
325	170	3	Slow
350	180	4	Moderate
375	190	5	
400	200	6	Moderately Hot
425	220	7	Fairly Hot
450	230	8	Hot
475	240	9	Very Hot
500	250	10	Extremely Hot

Any broiling recipes can be used with the grill of the oven, but beware of high-temperature grills.